COVID Survivors Kinot

Maḥberet Avodat Hashem

Esther Kruman

Editor

COVID Survivors Kinot

Maḥberet Avodat Hashem

Esther Kruman, Editor

Book Design, Él-Ad Eliovson

<u>Cover Photo</u>:
"Sunset in Jerusalem", by Mikhail Levit
By License from the Photographer

For questions, comments or feedback on the subject matter
email: info@partnersinprayer.live

For bulk orders or related information email:
reflexion101@gmail.com

First Printing: 2020

To my esteemed wife

Debbie

All the notes that I have since 1971,
with valuable lessons and insights from many Holy
Sefarim, extraordinary teachers, and inspiring role
models, were saved in my
Maḥberet Avodat Hashem,
my Service of God Notebook.

I learned how to transform these notebooks
from personal notes to practical applications
from you, to whom these words are dedicated.

What is the Source for a
Maḥberet Avodat Hashem?

רבינו תם
ספר הישר יג

כל הבא לעבוד עבודת הא'ל ולקבל עליו עול יראתו באמת, צריך תחילה
שיהיה לו ספר כולל זכרון נפלאות הבורא יתברך, לרשעים, ונסיו
לצדיקים, וספור גבורותיו ונוראותיו, כגון "אזר נא כנגד חלציך ואשאלך
והודיעני" (איוב לח:ג) וכל הפסוקים אשר אחריו. וישוב עליו לחזק
בשבועה לקרותו פעם אחת בשבוע בנחת וכוונה, וישים לבו לכל ענייניו.
כי הוא יהיה לטוטפות בין עיניו.

Rabbeinu Tam
The Book of the Upright #13

All who wish to enter into the service of the Almighty and
to receive upon oneself the yoke of His Awe in Truth,
must first have for themselves a recollection notebook of
the wonders of the Creator, may He be blessed: the
destructive things (that occurred), His miracles for
tzadikim, and a recounting of His Mighty Acts and His
Wonders. For example: "Gird up now thy loins like a
man; for I will inquire of you and you will respond to Me"
(Iyov 38:3) and all the subsequent verses. One should
review this and strengthen oneself with a vow to read it
once a week in a calm state and with concentration and
pay note to all its ideas. For it will be as a stimulator for
our vision.

הסכמת הרב יחיאל בר-לב שליט"א

מחבר ספרי ידיד נפש על הזהר הקודש, ש"ס ירושלמי וש"ס בבלי ועוד

בס"ד

לכבוד ידידי הגאון שליט"א

ידידי רב אבא יסבא בחמידא אלימלך הקריא לפני, כמה פרקים מספר שכתב הגאון הרב הגאון רב שמחה ונערב שיחיה לאורך ימים, דבר אחרי שהרך ונערב שיומשי דברים בה ושיחתנו כמה וכמה פעמים על נושאים שונים וכו...

ואמרתי לעצמי מאין נבעה שהרך ונערב יודע את רעיונותיו דל הכתב? הרגשתי שכלן העמוקים וחמודים כאשר חכמי שהרך ונערב לא אתפרסמ ברבים.

ורפושי שאמרתי את הדברים היקרים הללו דבר שהוליא חושב, אמרתי דלי שכתבו הספר [...] גדולה ונשמחה דאתן יום.

יתן ה' שהך שמחה ישמיע לאילה ספרים מתוך כל שלוחה וישבה אל דלי ישראל לאמונ ולהכין את הדעת רעיונא בערב...

ידידו וכו' יחיאל...

יחיאל אברהם בן רבי בנימין הלוי דנ[...]

Partners in Prayer

Partners in Prayer evolved to become Partners in Personal Development. We envision Partners using their connections through prayer to strategically pray for each other.

Rabbi Chaim Goldberger, our rabbinic guide, the author of *The Six Steps of Bitaḥon*, and a superb Partner in Torah, Prayer, and Development, teaches that we should use Partners in Bitaḥon to help us process the necessary steps of true *bitaḥon*.

We, a group of Partners in Torah, Personal Development, Bitaḥon, and Prayer, have been inspired to use the COVID Crisis, when many are first turning to prayer or first recognizing how prayer offers a comprehensive toolbox for all aspects of life, as a filing system for all we learn and experience to support others in mastering the Art of Prayer. We are assiduously working at collecting insights and experiences and using prayer to apply and reify. We are also organizing groups of Partners and Mentors to help people refine insights and identify places in prayer that address our unusual experiences. This project is our third offering, an invitation to take full advantage of one of our growing lists of Partners or one of our esteemed mentors.

Harav Yochanan Zweig *Shlitah* gave his blessing for this project.

Please visit www.partnersinprayer.live

Preface

It is with great excitement that I add my blessings to the sacred endeavor that has become the Partners in Tefillah series. From the instant I was asked to participate, I was able to sense the vibrations of energy ready to propel this project to great heights, and I immediately recognized the match between the moment at hand and the material that was going to be produced.

This is not to say that this particular assignment did not raise hesitations. I have long been troubled by the idea of preparing prayer materials for the Tisha B'Av kinot. Are we not confident that God will bring an end to our exile—now, this year? What does it say about our *bitaḥon*—our trust in God and His salvation—that we prepare words of comfort and mourning for yet another Tisha B'Av, as if to say, "We are probably going to be needing this material again this year?" Maybe we should refuse to write commentary on kinot, and dare God, as it were, to put us through another year of fasting and bitter remembrance!

But I think we can acquire a crucial perspective from the prophecies of Yirmiyahu. Yirmiyahu wrote vivid descriptions of the destruction of the Beit HaMikdash, descriptions that constitute a large portion of the dirges we recite on Tisha B'Av. He portrays visions of Jerusalem in ruins and the Jewish community decimated. But none of it had happened yet! It was all visions of what would happen in the future. What was Yirmiyahu doing? Why was he speaking about such catastrophes and virtually inviting them to happen?

Actually, what Yirmiyahu was doing was the opposite. He was opening our eyes to the pain being felt by the Shechinah. More than saying, "This is what will happen to us," the prophet was saying, "This is how God sees us now." He sees that our proud exterior is masking a ghastly core—a core made up of crumbling moral fiber and profound spiritual disconnect. That core stares back at Him and causes Him to see the Beit HaMikdash in flames and the nation in ruins. And if we could just allow ourselves to see that pain, perhaps we could still reverse course and arrest the path of disintegration.

COVID-19 has given us all a chance to see the Shechinah's pain. God has banished us from our shuls, from our schools and yeshivot, from the guests we used to have in our homes, from seeing one another's faces. He has taken away our health, our confidence, and our loved ones. His agony, as it were, has been on vivid display. But He is also engaged, as these words are written, in bringing recovery, in strengthening the survivors, in giving us reborn hope. Perhaps by our willingness to feel the pain that was so great as to have caused Him to bring this scourge upon our world, we can avert further tragedies too unspeakable to contemplate.

We prepare prayers for Tisha B'Av and commentaries on kinot not to anticipate another year of mourning, but to find new ways to sensitize ourselves to the suffering the loss of our spiritual glory brings to the Almighty. And if we can succeed in bringing one another to feel it just enough, there is no doubt we can make this be the year all our commentaries turn out to be unneeded.

Rabbi Chaim Goldberger
Partners in Prayer

Table of Contents

Preparatory Thoughts

The Futility of Our Words

I hate the whole race. There is no believing a word they say—your professional poets, I mean—there never existed a more worthless set than Byron and his friends for example. Poets praise fine sentiments and never practice them.

—Duke of Wellington, 1810

Here we are, about to begin this study of the kinot, poetic compositions that strive to guide us as we mourn the destructions of the Batei Mikdash, the Holy Temples in Jerusalem, and the exiles that followed. These words will take us across Jewish history, from the First Temple to the Second, from Jerusalem to Beitar, from Germany to York, England, from pogroms to the Holocaust. Yet how is it possible to feel anything other than the Futility of Our Words?

Yirmiyahu taught us, "You have covered Yourself with a cloud, so that prayer should not pass through" (Eichah 3:44). Today, God conceals Himself in the Heavens to keep out the words of our prayers. How, then, can we approach the kinot, the words of the great poets who were still lesser than the composers of our futile prayers?

Our only hope to combat this futility is to carefully study the kinot, searching for parallels to our own lives and the practical lessons that they offer us. This year, in the wake of the Coronavirus, those parallels seem even more readily apparent. Let us take this opportunity to uncover our living connection to our heritage, tragedies and triumphs alike. If God has concealed Himself, perhaps it is up to us to reveal Him.

We have the ability to empower the kinot with our study, so that their words will not be futile, but will instead stimulate thought and growth. If we can empower the words of the kinot, we may yet find a way to empower the words of our prayers.

An Assembly Place in Time

Ḥayim Greenberg used his 1951 address to the World Zionist Congress in Jerusalem to publicly challenge the Zionist movement and American Jews to rethink the nature of the relationship between Israel and America. To drive home his point, he deliberately addressed the Congress in Yiddish, as published in *Jewish Frontier*:

> *In a sense, one may say that the Jews have for many centuries, throughout the so-called Diaspora period, lived more in the sphere of time than in the sphere of space, or perhaps more in the sphere of music than in the sphere of the plastic.*

> *Plastic art is quite inconceivable apart from space. A painting, a sculptural or architectural work, must occupy room or ground; a melody is spaceless.*

> *In a symbolic sense, Jewish culture was more of the historical and musical type than of the geographic and plastic type.*

> *The Galut was perhaps the only example in history, at any rate, the most prominent example, of an ex-territorial civilization.*

Upon vast expanses of time and apparently out of nothing more than memories, strivings, and aspirations, our people created such grand structures as the Babylonian Talmud, the palaces of Kabbalah and Hasidism, the gardens of medieval Jewish philosophy and poetry, the self-discipline and inspirational ritualism of the Shulchan Aruch, the color and aroma of Sabbaths and holidays.

We were without territory, yet possessed of clear and fixed boundaries that Jews devotedly guarded; without armies—and yet so much heroism; without a Temple—and yet so much sanctity; without a priesthood—and yet each Jew, in effect, a priest; without kingship—and yet with such unexcelled spiritual "sovereignty."

Should we be ashamed of the exile? I am proud of it, and if Galut was a calamity (who can pretend it was not?), I am proud of what we were able to perform in that calamity. Let others be ashamed of what they did to us in exile.

Greenberg's words, describing our ability to live in this sphere of time rather than space, or what he describes as the sphere of music, remind me of the following verse and how we apply our reading of it: "My Master has spurned all my mighty men in the midst of me. He has called an assembly against me to crush my young men. My Master has trodden the virgin, the daughter of Yehudah, as in a winepress" (Eichah 1:15). We interpret "an assembly against me" as "a Festival against me," allowing halacha to define Tisha B'Av as a festival—so in the latter half of the day, we skip certain prayers that are never recited on a festival!

Our ability to transform the reading of a verse and treat it as a reality is exactly the magic that has allowed us to use this state of *galut*, exile, and transform it into those grand structures, palaces, and gardens with magnificent colors and aromas, as described by Greenberg above.

Yet here we are again, approaching Tisha B'Av in tragedy, suffering, and pain, without celebrating, honoring, or even paying attention to what we have accomplished in *galut*.

It is even more remarkable that the Book of Eichah, authored by Yirmiyahu the Prophet, was written years before the terrible tragedies of Tisha B'Av (Yirmiyahu 36:2–4)! Even before the Temple was destroyed by the Babylonians, even before the people suffered the violence of the exile, we were taught to cry over the Destruction.

Yirmiyahu sent a letter to the earliest exiles in Babylon urging them, "Build houses and settle; plant gardens and eat their produce. Take wives and beget sons and daughters; take wives for your sons and give your daughters to men and let them give birth to sons and daughters. Multiply there; do not let your numbers diminish. Seek the peace of the city to which I have exiled you and pray for it to God, for through its peace will you have peace" (29:6–7).

The same prophet who taught us to weep is the one who taught us how to *live*—how to build those magnificent structures, palaces, and gardens filled with poetry, colors and aromas. He taught us this before he wrote Eichah!

Is it possible that only those who know how to weep are able to transform any place in which they live into an Assembly Place in Time? Is this what the sages mean when they teach us that those who cry over the destruction will merit to see Jerusalem rebuilt? Is this what the Midrash means when it teaches us that, "On the day the Temple was destroyed the Mashiach was born" (Midrash Eichah Rabbati 1:57)?

Is this how Assaf, the psalmist, was able to sing about catastrophe: "A song of Assaf, O God! The nations have entered into Your estate, they defiled the Sanctuary of Your Holiness, they turned Jerusalem into a heap of rubble." (Tehillim 79:1) The midrash asks, "A song? This should be titled a Lamentation!"

We are taught that Assaf sang because God was merciful, directing His anger at the stones and beams of the Temple rather than at the Jews. Although the people of Israel were severely punished, only the Temple was destroyed; the nation survived (Rashi, Kiddushin 31b).

I don't know what it means when it says that God did not direct His anger at the Jews; we spend a great deal of time describing their horrible suffering. For me, the key phrase is, "the nation *survived*." Despite our horrible and tragic history, we have been granted the beautiful ability to not only survive, but to *thrive*.

This year, I hope that the kinot will reflect, not only our pain, but our recovery. Let us use the kinot to continue honoring our relationships with God and with each other. The tragedies befalling us are not limited to the past; we are presently grappling with deeply tragic and challenging circumstances. Yet we as a nation have generally responded in positive ways, with study, with unbelievable acts of kindness, with compassion. Let us use the kinot to continue honoring our relationships with God and with each other.

Only the one who fully appreciates the tragedy of our loss can honor our power to rebuild. We have transformed *galut* into the greatest intellectual, philosophical, and spiritual structures that exist in time, beyond space, keeping us connected even when we must remain physically apart. We live a life of music. It is *this* power that we use to build Israel, and it is with this power that we can build a world worthy of Redemption.

History as an Artichoke

We do not refer to the 9th of Av as the Hebrew date on which both Temples were destroyed. Instead we make lists: It was the date when the Children of Israel were sentenced to die out in the desert rather than enter the Promised Land. Beitar, the last stronghold of the Bar Kochba rebellion was destroyed in 133 CE. Turnus Rufus plowed up the area of the Temple and its surroundings. The Jews were expelled from Spain in 1492. (It wasn't actually on the *ninth* of Av, but that's another story.) World War I began on Tisha B'Av.

It's a long list and raises all sorts of dilemmas for the thinking person. Tisha B'Av forces us to confront the presence of evil in the world. We cannot revisit the Av stories without wondering how God can hide His face. We are urged to repent, but are not told what we must repair.

I often ask people who have just listened to a screaming cry for repentance, people who are careful in every aspect of their lives, for what they must repent. The answer is always the same: *"Everything!"* Perhaps Dostoyevsky was right when he wrote, "If Stavrogin believes, he does not think he believes. If he does not believe, he does not think he does not believe" (*The Possessed, or, The Devils*).

I returned home after one of those tirades—or as I would say, *menticides*—that moved people for a moment or two, but no more, because they did not know what they did and did not believe. The family, not I, was eating artichokes, and I had an epiphany as I watched them savor the multiple, prickly, and densely superimposed layers: Tisha B'Av can be better understood as an artichoke.

What if, rather than compile lists of all the terrible things that happened on Tisha B'Av, we examined each tragedy as one prickly layer to help us uncover the deep core of our beliefs?

This is what our people have done throughout history. When the generations of the spies died out, the Israelites renewed our covenant with God, committing to learn from the mistakes of the past and carry on our inherited legacy. We peeled back a layer, uncovered a new understanding, and were better prepared for the future. When we returned to Israel from Babylon and Persia, the Men of the Great Assembly renewed Torah and its applications, beginning a period of fantastic creativity and possibility. When the Second Temple was destroyed, Rabbi Yochanan ben Zakai saved Yavneh and her sages, and renewing the role of Torah in our lives. Each layer, prickly and painful, allowed us to achieve new heights.

We all may have beliefs, experiences, and emotional complexities that make it difficult to access the "core" of who we are. Our aim is not to remove each layer, reach a conclusion, and feel satisfied that we have uncovered the truth. This would be a state of intellectual stagnancy, which places the emphasis on what we think or know (or think we know) instead of what we *do*. Rather, our aim is to deepen our understanding of the experiences that layer us—from both our ancestral memory and our lived realities—and *use* our findings to move forward with renewed clarity, focus, empathy, and vigor.

What lessons have we learned from these trying times? What systemic problems have we identified in our communities? What is lacking in our familial and social relationships? What holes have we found inside ourselves?

Once we identify the problems, we must turn our attention on the solutions. What actions have we taken to remedy these challenges? What are we *doing* with what we learned? What have we gained from all this pain?

When I observe the conversations and kindnesses in our communities, I see us asking these questions and beginning to implement changes. We pay closer attention to our home lives, creating our own sacred spaces. We focus on self-development, taking courses and learning new skills. We repair relationships that we have neglected, sometimes reaching out to people for the first time in years. We protect those who are most vulnerable, whether it's a lonely friend or an elderly stranger. And we are kinder to ourselves, I hope, taking the time to center ourselves and prioritize our emotional wellbeing.

Take note of these changes. We should continue to learn and grow from these lessons as we cautiously venture into a semblance of normalcy, so that we can rebuild our communities into something stronger than they were before. We need to preserve our relationships with each other. We need to value our home lives and the caretakers (quite often women) who cultivate them. We need to be more inclusive, especially towards those who were isolated even before this pandemic. Our communal spaces and gatherings must be accessible to people with physical disabilities. Our leaders cannot overlook the importance of mental health when *paskening*, issuing judgments.

These are not new concerns. Many people have been navigating these challenges for years. I think that we can all now see the implicit danger and devastation that occurs when a person is left in the dark shadows of loneliness. Every single member of our communities deserves to be included and valued. Let us work together to facilitate that, creating meaningful opportunities for *everyone* among us whenever we gather in public spheres, and even when we are physically apart.

Eavesdropping

People often request copies of the recordings I made of my personal conversations with my father and Uncle Noach, *zt"l*. Even their casual comments were filled with treasures of wisdom, insight and clarity. The recordings contain many intensely private details and I am not willing to share them.

I am currently studying two complex topics in Halacha, Jewish law, and the books are piling up on my desk. I glanced at the stacks and realized that I have a book from practically every century since the closing of the Talmud. In fact, what I have on my desk is a recorded conversation between the Jewish People and God over the long course of our history. These are all public dialogues, often debates, and offer powerful insights into dealing with endless issues and challenges, conflicts external and internal.

Let me see: There are Responsa of the *Geonim* (late sixth century to mid-eleventh century Iraq), Talmudic insights of the Rif (Morocco, Tunisia, and Spain, 1013–1103), Rashi (Troyes, 1040–1105, during the Crusade of Godfrey), the Rambam (Cordoba and Egypt, 1135–1204—he served as the court physician to Sultan Saladin), the Rosh (Germany and Toledo, 1250–1328), Rabbi Joseph Caro (Toledo, Salonika, and Safed, 1488–1575), Rabbi Akiva Eiger (Hungary and West Prussia, 1761–1837), the Chafetz Chaim (Radun, then Poland, 1838–1933), Rav Moshe Feinstein (Belarus and Russia, 1895–1986, and twentieth-century America), and more.

Each book reflects the whole of Torah while offering insight into the society and struggles of each author. All the books written since Sinai are part of an ongoing conversation between God and Israel. Torah study invites us to eavesdrop on this ongoing dialogue.

We can listen to the discussions of rabbis dealing with the threats of their time, from Karaites and Crusaders. We hear them console people frightened of the Inquisition and Chmielnicki. The conversations cover Marranos and Moonies, clothing, marriage, childrearing, love, business, and God.

The Tisha B'Av kinot afford us headphones to listen into the intensely emotional talks that we have had with God since the destruction of the first Temple. It is painful, almost torturous, to listen in to these conversations, but there is great wisdom to be distilled, if only we will listen carefully.

The same goes for our current dialogue. This is a time of conversation between many of us, including those who are used to being disconnected from each other. Let us take this time to *listen*.

KINAH 1

Finding Joy

Gone is the joy of our hearts because the festival pilgrimage has been discontinued.

Rav Ḥisda said, "At first, when the fear of the Sanhedrin was upon Israel, lewd words were never inserted in songs, but when the Sanhedrin was abolished lewd words were inserted in songs."

Rabbi Yosi ben Avin said in the name of Rav Ḥisda, "At first, when adversity came upon Israel, they put a stop to rejoicing in the face of it. When the Sanhedrin ceased to function, song ceased from the places of feasting."

—Eichah Rabbah 5:15

When people ceased to come to Jerusalem for the three Festivals, we lost the Sanhedrin. When we lost the Sanhedrin, we lost the joy of our hearts. It seems clear that we must have a Sanhedrin in order to have joy, and that we must keep ourselves centered on a central place in order to merit the Sanhedrin. The Sanhedrin was able to focus all the Jews in their spiritual lives. They were able to keep the people unified. But the people had to be *committed* to being unified. When they ceased to travel to Jerusalem, the center of Jewish spiritual life, they lost their connection to the people as a unit. People were satisfied with their individual spiritual lives, yet disconnected from the nation as a whole. They defined their spiritual lives by their own terms. They did not see their connection to the entire nation as a necessary part of their religious and cultural life. They were able to exist on their own. But a self-defined spiritual life is constrained by one's own perceptions, knowledge, and limitations.

If the people had lived as part of the entire nation, their connection to God would have been unlimited. They would have nurtured each other, demanded more from each other, inspired each other, and challenged each other. They would have had the necessary humility in serving God if they had recognized that they were only one small part of a much larger whole. When a person defines the terms of his relationship with God, he is being arrogant. In a relationship with the Infinite Being, who should determine the parameters of the relationship? The Infinite or the very limited human being? A limited human being is ultimately an unhappy and frustrated human being. Thus, when they ceased to travel to Jerusalem, when they stopped connecting to the Jewish people, when they limited their relationship with God, they lost their sense of joy.

There are times when we cannot inhabit the same physical space, due to forces beyond our control. This situation forces us to reexamine what it means to be distant and disconnected. At such times, defiantly pursuing physical closeness is the act of a selfish, arrogant individual, for it jeopardizes the health and safety of our community. Distance is transformed to a selfless and communal act, a way to care for and protect our people. Yet we cannot let that physical distance come at the cost of our sense of togetherness. Instead, we devote our attention to *emotional* closeness, to strengthening the bonds that unite us, no matter where we are. Even when we are able to inhabit the same space, we must remember to nurture our emotional closeness. It is this tender connection, this keen awareness of what unites us, that ultimately gives us joy.

KINAH 3

The Forgotten

They, the soon to be forgotten, accurately suspected that they would be erased from the memory of the other tribes.

Reuven, Gad, and part of Menasheh returned home across the Jordan after an absence of fourteen years, fulfilling the commitment they made to Moshe in this week's portion (Numbers 32:31). "When they came near the Jordan, Reuven, Gad, and the half-tribe of Menasheh built a great altar to look upon there by the Jordan" (Yehoshuah 22:10). They wanted to provoke a response: "When Israel heard that they had built the altar, the whole assembly of Israel gathered at Shiloh to go to war against them."

A delegation of the leaders of Israel confronted them, "How could you betray the God of Israel like this? How could you turn away from Hashem and build yourselves an altar in rebellion against Him? …You are turning away from Hashem!" (Yehoshuah 22:16–18).

The two and a half tribes listened to the accusations and realized that the forgetting had begun. The delegation began with accusations, not a question. They were suspect, on the fringes of the nation, despite their many years fulfilling their word to Moshe.

"We did it for fear that someday your descendants might say to ours, 'What do you have to do with Hashem, the God of Israel? Hashem has made the Jordan a boundary between us and you! You have no share in Hashem.' ... That is why we said, 'Let us get ready and build an altar to be a witness between us and you and the generations that follow. Then in the future your descendants will not be able to say to ours, 'You have no share in Hashem.'" they said (Yehoshuah 22:24–27).

The delegation responded, "Today we know that Hashem is with us, because you have not been unfaithful to God in this matter" (Yehoshuah 22:31). The message failed. The proper response would have been, "We swear to never forget your share in Hashem."

The people of Israel were glad to hear the report and praised Hashem (Yehoshuah 22:33). They spoke no more of war, but a passive war, waged through forgetting those on the fringes, had already begun.

The two and a half tribes named the monumental altar, "A Witness Between Us—that Hashem is God." Once they understood that the delegation had failed to acknowledge their concerns, they could use the monument to mark their relationship with God. But it would never work to remind the tribes on the *other* side of the Jordan that they who lived on the other side were also part of Israel. They were forgotten and eventually forgot. They quickly faded from the mental map of Israel.

We remember our history during these days as we approach the Ninth of Av, the anniversary of the destruction of both the First and Second Temples, among other tragedies associated with this day. We even cry out to God, demanding, "Remember, Hashem, what has happened to us" (Eichah 5:1). Before listing what we remember and demanding that God remember, we should focus on those on the fringes whom we have forgotten and allowed to forget: the friend who is silently suffering whom we called once and then forgot. The poor person whose story broke our hearts and we then forgot. The child struggling with emotional issues, the one we didn't know how to help, the one we forgot and allowed to forget his roots. All of those on the fringes—singles, the divorced, the widowed, people searching for their identity, and the people who have difficulty "fitting in." Those who have faded from our mental maps.

We have a commandment to place *tzitzit*, fringes, on our four-cornered garments, so men wear four-cornered garments to obligate ourselves to tie the fringes at all times. All corners of the world, everywhere, but especially those on the fringes, "so that you may remember and perform all My commandments and be holy to your God" (Numbers 15:40).

We cannot possibly perform His commandments or be holy to God when we fail to remember those on the fringes. Men constantly wear *tzitzit* because monuments fade and dim. All of us, men and women alike, include the mitzvah of *tzitzit* in our daily recitation of the Shema.

This period of mourning communities lost is the time for building communities that will never be forgotten for their commitment to remember each person. Or *re*building, as we are now. We must remember the vulnerable and the marginalized, the lonely and the destitute, the sick and the elderly, and anyone at all who feels ostracized or lost or disconnected. Those who have the privilege to build have the obligation to *tie*—to reach out to every single person on the fringes, pull them close, and tightly unite us all.

KINAH 4

The Hovering Life

This need to spit the world's sinister truth in its face is as old as the world itself. Robert Musil wrote in *The Man Without Qualities* (one of the most difficult books I've ever read), "One can't resent one's era without being swiftly punished by it." Ulrich, an Austrian mathematician, is in search of a sense of life and reality, but he fails to find it. His ambivalence towards morals and indifference to life has brought him to the state of being "a man without qualities," depending on the outer world to form his character. His most typical attitude is a keenly analytical passivity. His intention is to arrive at a synthesis between strict scientific fact and the mystical, which he refers to as "the hovering life."

We lose our personal qualities when we depend on others to form our character; we become People Without Qualities.

This next kinah, based on Yeḥezkel 23, describes the debate between Samaria and Jerusalem. You will find that the people of both Yehudah and the Northern Kingdom were caught up in a game of comparisons—a game that caused both to lose their better qualities.

Sometimes there is a pressure to define ourselves in relation to others. It is important to take the time to reflect on who you are, not as someone divorced from your people and your culture, but as someone with unique qualities, gifts, and emotional complexities. We have all had different ways of coping with this pandemic. We should recognize that it isn't a competition, that we are allowed to have different needs during this time. We can and should learn from each other, but we also need to learn from ourselves. And by taking care of ourselves, we are better able to care for each other.

The Ripped Coat

Rabbi Ḥaninah bar Papah began his lecture on Eichah with the verse, "As one who removes his garment in cold weather, and as vinegar upon natron, so is one who sings songs upon a sorrowful heart" (Mishlei 25:20). Rabbi Ḥaninah and Rabbi Yoḥanan both say, "What did the Ten Tribes and the tribes of Yehudah and Binyamin resemble? Two men who were both wrapped in the same new coat on a winter's day. One pulled one way and on pulled the other way until they ripped it. Similarly, the Ten Tribes did not cease worshiping idols in Samaria and the tribes of Yehudah and Binyamin were serving them in Jerusalem. Jerusalem was not to be destroyed until they caused Jerusalem to be destroyed (Midrash Eichah, Introduction XII Part I).

Both rabbis are comparing Jerusalem to the winter coat that person wears to protect him from the cold. Neither the Ten Tribes, nor the tribes of Yehudah and Binyamin, appreciated the protection that Jerusalem afforded them. Both nations were focused on ripping off their coat; both wanted to shed Jerusalem and all it represented. Little did they realize that by losing Jerusalem, they were losing their protection.

The analogy describes two men sharing the same coat. We can assume that these men were too poor to afford their own coats. Poor and vulnerable, their shared coat was so uncomfortable that they were willing to rip it off in spite of the bitter cold. Each pulled at the coat, forgetting that the coat was shared. The men were so close, wearing the same garment, both feeling the same discomfort, both so bothered by the itch of the material. Their experiences were so similar to each other, and yet, in their discomfort, each forgot that the garment would be torn if they did not work together and share it.

We are not simply describing people who forgot that Jerusalem afforded protection. We are discussing people who are incredibly similar to each other, people with shared experiences and circumstances, people who battle these same issues even while wearing the same "coat." And yet, by rejecting the coat, they forget each other. People who shared so much, were so bothered by what Jerusalem represented, and how they experienced Jiving in the presence of Jerusalem that they ceased to connect to each other.

Perhaps it was this break between people who shared so much that was the true cause of the loss of the protection of Jerusalem.

When we read Kinah 4 on Tisha B'Av night and speak of the debate between the Ten Tribes and Jerusalem, we are describing people who were so lost and so uncomfortable and so focused on shedding the demands of living with a Jerusalem, that they ceased to connect to each other.

We can have numerous people who share many of the same concerns, and yet when deciding how to best respond, each party is so focused on their approach that they forget the connection they share with others who approach the same issues differently. If one party says, "The internet is evil and must be rejected," or, "A wife must wear only *this* hair covering," they assume that anyone who chooses a different approach must not share their same concerns. They are ripping away at the coat that wraps us all together.

It is this ripping of the coat that causes us to forfeit the protection of Jerusalem. It is not enough to respect each other as individuals. We must respect our *community* and remember who we are as a unit. We have all been trying to get through time, and it is true that we have different ways of doing so. But we cannot lose sight of *why* we are doing it. We cannot let our differences rip us apart. We can only protect ourselves and each other when we remember to protect us all.

KINAH 6

Moments in Time

"Everything came to a standstill."

Shavat. This is based on Kinah 5:15: "Gone, *shavat*, is the joy of our hearts, our dancing has turned into mourning." The Ibn Ezra explains that the "joy of our hearts" refers to the offerings brought in the Temple, as in Yeḥezkel: "And you, Son of Man, behold, on the day that I take their stronghold from them, the joy of their glory, the darling of their eyes, and the exaltation of their soul, their sons and their daughters" (24:25).

The imagery of this prophecy begins with the death of Yeḥezkel's wife (Yeḥezkel 24:15–27). One moment she is there, and the next moment, she is gone. The darling of his eyes was taken away in an instant. His life was shattered. "Won't you tell us what these acts that you are doing mean for us?" (Yeḥezkel 24:19). People did not understand Yeḥezkel's response to such a tragedy. They could only understand that the prophet was sending a message to them.

Our lives can change in a moment. Our world can stop. There is nothing we can do but watch. Those of us who are old enough remember exactly what we were doing and where we were at the moment we heard of the planes crashing into the World Trade Center on 9/11. Time seemed to stop at that

41

moment. Yeḥezkel was telling his people that they were functioning in Babylon with the assumption that the Temple was still standing and that sacrifices were still being offered. They still relied on that protection. He was warning them that their world would change in a single moment; a moment that they knew, but refused to believe, was coming. Afterwards, nothing would be the same.

Our lives can change in a single moment. The world is entirely different from one minute to the next. It can happen for good, as with the *az* (as in *Az Yashir*) of the Splitting of the Sea, or it can happen in a negative way, as with the loss of the Altar and sacrifices.

This year, the world changed for all of us. Perhaps we followed the news with an increasing sense of dread, or perhaps we felt that the virus was far away, that we were untouchable, that everything would resolve itself on its own. Then everything changed, and we watched as the entire world stopped in its tracks. Suddenly, the entire fabric of our social reality seemed to rip apart at the seams. The little treasures we once took for granted, such as fresh produce or a friendly handshake, became dangerous. So too, we lost the joys of our ritual life, from praying at shul with a minyan to studying at yeshiva. And there is nothing we can do but watch. We cannot reverse what has happened; we can only adjust to our new reality, for as long as it lasts.

Clinging to the Past

Late one evening, a grief counselor spoke to a man in hospice. The patient was suffering from ALS (Lou Gehrig's disease). "What's the hardest part of this experience for you?" the therapist asked. "The hospitalization? The disease?"

"No," the dying man replied. "The hardest part is that everyone sees me in the past tense. Something that once was. No matter what's going on with my body, I will still be a whole person. There is a part of me that is not definable and doesn't change, that I will not lose and does not disappear with age or disease. There is a part of myself that I cling to. That is who I am and that is who I will always be."

The way that we who mourn on Tisha B'Av experience the subsequent Seven Weeks of Consolation indicates that we see ourselves as something that once was and is no more. We recover from Tisha B'Av rather quickly. I am a committed *simcha* (happiness) person, and not advocating that we suffer for the next seven weeks. But it sure is strange that we have seven full weeks of consolation that we don't need! Did we miss something in our mourning? How can we recover so quickly when the Sages were certain we would need almost two months to return to ourselves?

We mourn the past, the Jerusalem that once was, the great nation that we were so long ago. We tell old stories and weep over the countless tragedies of our history. We mourn in the past tense, so we recover quickly. I needed a long time to reconnect with life after my father's passing. I don't need to recover when I observe his *yahrtzeit*, the anniversary of his death. Tisha B'Av has become an elaborate yahrtzeit of a long-ago death, and we don't need seven weeks to recover.

That is exactly what I mourned this past Tisha B'Av: I ached for people who see Judaism in the past tense, whether it is the Jerusalem of old, the great Jewish communities of Europe and Spain, or even how much better things were a generation ago. I cried for the people who do not believe that there is a part of us that doesn't change no matter where or when we live. I weep for those who forget that each of us is indefinable, special, beautiful, magnificent. I mourn for those who see the world through the eyes of our suffering, not our greatness. I agonize for a nation that doesn't pride itself on its ability to keep Jerusalem alive two thousand years after its destruction by the Romans. I mourn those who are stuck in the past tense without any joy in the present. The ache does not disappear with the end of the fast. The pain is palpable. The hurt remains. I need Seven Weeks of Consolation.

We started ***www.partnersinprayer.live*** because we refuse to cling to the past. We cling to the present and future. We do not want to be another website that shares the insights of previous generations without rejoicing in their practical applications for ours. Our goal was, and is, to delve into the wealth of a living Torah and discover treasures of meaningful wisdom. All who contribute write and teach for those who study to discover their indefinable potential, not

44

for those who simply want to keep the past alive. We are not a dying body. We are a living being. Whole. Magnificent. Eternal.

I find my consolation in choosing to live in the Present Tense.

KINAH 7

Above the Stars

In this kinah, Hashem only seems to focus on the bad things in our relationship with Him. But what about all the good? If the positive aspects of a relationship are not acknowledged, we begin to feel neglected and taken for granted. Our accomplishments, all the good things we've done, seem to lose their power. Perhaps worst of all, the next time that we achieve something good, we no longer know if we can trust our feelings of accomplishment and joy.

This kinah helps us reconnect to our special moments with Hashem. Thus, the first thing we say is, "You do not remember the *Brit Bein HaB'tarim*, the Covenant Between the Pieces." What was the gift of this covenant? Hashem promised Avraham that He would always provide his descendants with the means of living above the stars.

This was not a promise to always save the Jewish people. We do not pray with the mindset that it will secure our fate; we cannot passively rely on the belief that Hashem will swoop in and rescue us. Hashem's promise was to give *us* the means to raise *ourselves* above the stars. He acknowledged our potential and future accomplishments, empowering us to make our own reality.

46

None of us can consistently live at such a high level, but we can connect to the times when we did experience life above the stars. We can say to Hashem, "You've kept Your promise before. Now do it again."

Here is a *tikkun,* a positive action, that one can take from Tisha B'Av: When we do mitzvot, are they a process of self-discovery? Or are we merely doing them because everyone else does, and this is what we do? Community is important, yes, and we should honor our traditions. Yet Avraham's covenant gave us more than endurance. It gave us the ability to lift ourselves to new heights. Yiddishkeit directs us, nurtures us, nourishes our growth and development. This is what the Vilna Gaon describes as "discovering your flag."

What does it mean to say that Hashem used "the wings of eagles?" He did not send magical birds to carry us through the skies. Rashi interprets this as the moment we left Egypt. When the Israelites united for the Paschal Offering, how was it that there was no fighting or shoving in line or mass chaos? After all, Moshe didn't give them specific instructions for how to organize this. Yet somehow, everyone had a sense of where they needed to be, how to get there, and what actions to take when they did. It was a moment of perfect harmony, absent of all the little tensions that typically arise when many people attempt the same task.

Herein lies the magic of "the wings of eagles." Everyone understood what was meant of them and felt content with their lot. This is how it feels to be carried through the sky on eagles' wings—for every Jew to move freely and peacefully towards our unified destination. And this is the feeling that we are supposed to experience when Mashiach comes. There will be no need for debate about who is right, who is wrong, or who is better than whom. There will be no fighting, no shoving, no chaos—just respect and dignity, *kavod* and *malchut*.

So too, this is how our relationship is meant to be with Hashem, and how it was when the Temple was first built. Not on our passive reliance on Him, nor a passive reliance on each other. We can especially see this now, in these difficult times. We can no longer depend on our community, shul, or beit midrash to give us a space for God in our lives. We need to create that space ourselves. As we have hopefully learned, each of us must reflect on what we can offer to bring us all closer to life above the stars.

Rendezvous with Time

"And You did not remember the assembly place You designated for Your followers."

We refer to each of the festivals as a *mo'ed,* a Meeting Place in Time (see "An Assembly Place in Time"). We even refer to Tisha B'Av as a *mo'ed,* applying certain laws of the Festivals after midday.

However, there is an aspect of this Meeting Place in Time that troubles me. There is a custom to avoid certain things from the beginning of the Three Weeks until after Tisha B'Av. Many people delay surgery or business deals during the period, which does not bother me. What I find troublesome is when people enter the Three Weeks expecting bad things to occur. Some people even wonder if they can pray for a miracle, or anything good at all, because they see the Three Weeks as a fixed period when only bad things can happen.

It was certainly a tragedy when the assembly place God designated for His followers was destroyed. However, perhaps it was a hint that it was now possible for us to designate places on our own. The Sages, immediately following the destruction of the Second Temple, taught us how to transform every place we gather for prayer into a miniature Sanctuary. They took the loss of a single designated place as an opportunity to learn how to create many such designated places.

This takes us back to the Tabernacle, the original Temple in the desert, which did not have a designated place, meaning one specific place in the desert, but wherever it was erected by the people, the building became the place. The building constructed by the people is where we found the Divine Presence. By introducing the idea of a designated place, we were empowered to create such places ourselves. We do not do so to replace the Temple. We see each of our own "temples" as a brick in the construction of the Third Temple.

If we can do it with a place, why can we not do the same with time? Why can we not begin to see this time of year as an opportunity? When did we ever accept limitations placed on our creative powers?

If we approach the Three Weeks as an unchanging time, we are making the same mistake as the generation sentenced to die in the desert over the course of forty years. That generation made no attempt to change the decree. That generation did not access all their experiences—from the bringing of the Paschal Offering to the Splitting of the Sea, from Sinai to constructing the Tabernacle—to realize that every experience had been to empower them to change their reality. They accepted that they would die out in the desert. They made no effort to change the time.

Why do we pray on Tisha B'Av for Redemption, for the rebuilding of Jerusalem, for the destruction of evil, for the Mashiach, if we act as if this time is fixed? How can we pray if we do not act as if our prayers can bring about the greatest miracles and transform this from a day of tragedy into a day of infinite celebration?

When God did not remember His designated assembly place, it served as a reminder for *us*, of all that He has empowered us to accomplish. We should not perpetuate bad times by giving up on the possibility of good times. Even in bad circumstances, we have the opportunity to create good things. This is especially the case during the Coronavirus pandemic, when all of us are davening privately. Our self-designated assemblies are not just the shuls and the *batei midrashim* and yeshivos, but our homes. Every home has become a brick in the Third Temple.

God's Anger

This kinah describes our experience of God's anger as something that builds up and eventually erupts. He continually warns us, "If you do this, I'll get angry." Yet it seems that each time we transgress, Hashem represses His anger, until He finally releases it all at once. Our first Temple is destroyed, our cities are destroyed, our entire reality is destroyed… This was not the anger of a single moment. We seem to have experienced centuries of pent-up fury. How can this be?

According to the Gemara Avodah Zarah, Hashem releases His anger for one second every day, so as not to let it build up over time. But we know of a period during which Hashem did not release His anger. This was when Bilaam wanted to curse the Israelites. Bilaam would wait each day for Hashem's anger, thinking that he could outsmart Him and seize those moments to curse us. Instead, Hashem suppressed His anger to protect us from Bilaam's curse.

However, Hashem is not a human being. Surely He does not *need* these moments of anger, as He does not need anything. And even in the midst of His "anger"—which is in itself a human emotion that we attribute to Him to help us understand Him—how could Divine Wrath possibly indicate a lack of control? If Hashem did not want Bilaam to curse us, He could prevent it without suppressing His anger.

Bilaam did not discover a moment of Divine "vulnerability" to successfully curse the Israelites. Rather, Bilaam weaponized Hashem's anger by directing their attention to it. This lead Bnei Yisrael astray, thereby *eliciting* Hashem's anger through their own actions.

If you are afraid that someone will lose control and explode at any moment, it destroys your relationship. When someone is in a fit of rage, they do not concentrate on the good experiences you have shared together. All your cherished memories of love and happiness are suddenly in jeopardy. As the one fearing that outburst, you lose your sense of trust and security. You may feel an impulse to withdraw from your relationship. You might even express your own anger. You *distance* yourself.

Bilaam cursed our relationship with God by poisoning it with this element of anger. When we conceive God's anger as an explosion of repressed rage, *that* is Bilaam's curse.

We did not need to experience God's anger when we had the Beit HaMikdash. Every time we went astray, we brought Him sacrifices to immediately make amends. This helped nurture our relationship with Hashem and keep us close to Him.

We see the importance of this dynamic right in the beginning of the Torah, when Adam and Ḥavah ate from the Tree of Knowledge. They know that they did wrong and then they hear the Voice of God "walking in the garden." Instead of approaching Hashem and dealing with the issue right away, they hide from Him. This was the real "sin" of the Garden of Eden—not eating from the tree, for which they could have repented, but running away from Hashem instead of taking the opportunity to nurture their relationship.

The Temple was a place for us to confront Hashem and resolve any outstanding issues in our relationship. But we were so afraid of His anger that we neglected to do so. We fled from Him and kept our distance, tragically, creating a Bilaam-type anger that never had to be there.

We all know how damaging it is to distance ourselves from our loved ones. The fear of losing each other may lead us to act rashly or to emotionally withdraw, as if this could shield us from the pain of being apart. Now is not a time to say, "God must be angry with us," nor is it a time to say, "God must be angry with the world." No matter how frightening and unstable our circumstances seem to be, we can still find ways to nurture our relationships from afar. Bad times need not rob us of good memories. So let us remember how important we are to each other. Let us remind each other of the love and joy between us, and the love and joy will still be there, keeping us close in our hearts.

KINAH 8

Possibility Gatherers

I love many forms of music, but I have not been blessed with any musical skills. I love literature, but I struggled to read Proust. I love books about mathematics, but I do not have a mathematical mind. I love art, but I am not artistic. I love fiction, but I have not written a short story since I was seven years old. I love refinishing old furniture, but I have not done any of that sort of work since 1984. I love to ski, but I am not very good at it. I love photography, but my finger finds its way into every picture. I love watching a computer genius at work, but I will never completely master Word.

I am not frustrated by any of the above, because I love the adventure of life. I cannot claim to be exceptionally good at living life, but the joy offered by so many possibilities is enough for me to feel that life is good. I guess you can call me a Possibility Gatherer.

I loved learning with my grandfather, *zt"l*, even though I did not have his knowledge or memory. I loved spending time with Rav Yaakov Kaminestky, *zt"l*, even though I was not as righteous as he was. I loved studying with my father, *zt"l*, even though I knew that I could not read a text with as much insight as did he. I loved and love being with great people because they reflected the possibilities of life. The possibilities are sufficient to make me happy. I rejoice in being a Possibility Gatherer.

The most powerful moment of Tisha B'Av for me is midday, when I can rise from sitting in a mourner's position on the floor and sit on a regular chair. The Temple continued to burn, but we shed a small part of our mourning in the middle of the day because Yirmiyahu refers to Tisha B'Av as a *mo'ed,* a holiday. The prophet is describing our enemies' rejoicing when they destroyed Jerusalem, but the Sages grab hold of that "*Mo'ed*" and refuse to let go. They declared Tisha B'Av to have some elements of a holiday (see "Assembly Place in Time").

The Sages wanted us to rise from the ground and limit our mourning *even when the Temple was still burning.* They wanted us to see the possibilities of life on the saddest day of the Jewish calendar. Even in mourning, we must always look to the promise of life. Mourning is not the natural state of a human being. Joyous adventure is ours for the taking. We are not survivors and sufferers; we are Possibility Gatherers, even on Tisha B'Av.

I recall a quote from Rabbi Joachim Prinz, posted in the United States Holocaust Memorial: "To be a Jew was now a new discovery, and to emphasize one's Jewishness in the face of danger and disgrace became the thing to do."

Only a Possibility Gatherer would discover "The Thing To Do" while suffering in Nazi Germany. Only Possibility

Gatherers could build the modern State of Israel from the ashes of the Holocaust.

I don't know if the world has ever stopped burning. There are so many destructive forces, from the disease inflicting us now to the recent Australian wildfires to the negative emotions that we feel towards each other and ourselves. It is up to us to extinguish these flames and flood the world with our own positive light.

There is only one question we must ask ourselves on Tisha B'Av: Can we still see the possibilities of life? I can. I invite you to help me pick up all the possibilities I am busy gathering.

Lacking or Desire

There is an important Rashi commentary on the second story of Creation that teaches us an essential idea about prayer. The original verse reads, "Now all the trees of the field were not yet on the earth and all the herb of the field had not yet sprouted, for Hashem, God, had not sent rain upon the earth and there was no man to work the soil" (Bereishit 2:5). Rashi explains, "There was no one to recognize the benefit of the rains. When Adam came and knew that rain was necessary for the world, he prayed for them and they fell."

In *Da'at Tefillah*, one of the best works I have read on prayer, Rabbi Ehud Avi Tzedek derives from this Rashi that we must pray as "Lackers," which is to say, as people who have a need: "Adam recognized that the creation lacked rain, and therefore prayed for it." The idea, primarily based on the Maharal, is that we must always approach God as "beggars." We are lacking in everything, and most of all, we lack the opportunity to live in a perfected creation, unified in God.

Da'at Tefillah is not alone in reading Rashi this way. It is the same reading that I have heard and read my entire life. However, I cannot find the word "lacking" anywhere in Rashi's comment! I only see Rashi describing the first step as "recognizing the benefit of rain." I believe that Rashi is offering an entirely different approach to prayer—that of *Desire*.

Rashi describes a person who recognizes that more benediction and Divine Sustenance is available. The person appreciates the potential, promise, and benefit of the "good," using prayer to express his desire (also known as *nefesh*). We say to God, "We see that there is more. We see that it is good. We desire that good."

Whenever I hear someone urging us to repent, I hear a stress on what we lack. Rashi's approach to teshuvah is to express our desire for more; to live at a higher level, to attach even more to God.

The first question we are asked by the Heavenly Tribunal is, "*Tzipita l'Yeshua?* Did you wait for the Redemption?" The Lacker waits for Redemption by focusing on a world that is lacking. He waits in his need. The Desirer does not sit and wait in his need; he works hard to fulfill a desire for a better and more complete world. Rashi's form of Service is to connect with our nefesh, our passionate desire for more, and express that desire in our prayer.

Prayer is a call for action. When we see what is missing in the world, we should not simply dwell on its absence. Rather, we should envision what the world *could* be and take steps to bring about Redemption.

I use the Nine Days to express my desire to live in a redeemed world in which my soul can live at its highest level. I offer my desire, not my lackings, to God, with hope and confidence. It is thus that my prayers are considered as Offerings on the Altar.

Between Hope & Despair

There are moments when the programmed heaviness of the Nine Days and Tisha B'Av suck the air from my heart in rhythmic assonance with aimless conversations. It's that point in deep talk when I shudder at the limitations of words, the flash of ague that burns when I suspect the futility of ideas to shatter the problems discussed. I chant the kinot, sharing my fifty years of Tisha B'Av weeping, convinced that I empathize with Yirmiyahu who warned and pled, who wept and challenged his people, only to observe his efforts mix and disappear with the smoke rising from the burning Temple.

Evagrius Ponticus, a fourth-century monk, would describe such a Tisha B'Av experience as *acedia*, defined by Kathleen Norris as "the sadness, the disgust with life, which comes from a much deeper source—our inability to get along *with ourselves*, our disunion *with God*" (*Acedia & Me: A Marriage, Monks, and a Writer's Life*). Jerusalem was lost, say the Sages, because of our inability to get along. The loss of the Temple is a disunion with God. It leads us to question the tangible results of mourning the tragedies of Jewish history. We've been crying and praying for two millennia. Despite our survival—the miraculous return to Israel and the waves of her accomplishments that rush out declaring, "We are alive and well, thriving, changing, aspiring to more!"—we mourn these Nine Days as we did when hiding in the Judean hills watching the Romans level Jerusalem, trembling before the violent Crusades, and crammed into German cattle cars. There are no official words during the day that allow us to appreciate the good, and I wonder whether we've been infected by Tisha B'Av acedia.

I ask children and adults whether they believe that their prayers to rebuild Jerusalem will change anything, whether their mourning the Temple will speed its return. The answer is always, whether firm or in whispered sadness, *no*. "Do you experience your mitzvot bringing hope and beauty to the world?" I ask, and I hear the same *no*. I grew up with teachers, many of whom were Holocaust survivors, constantly speaking of Jewish suffering, and their words left hollow spaces in my heart. I too taste our infinite pain, but I nourish my soul with the joyous possibilities of serving God. I cannot believe that we are meant to experience dangerously infectious acedia, especially since the original Tisha B'Av was a response to "Crying in Acedia," hopeless tears. The festival's observances were designed to battle the infection, not to spread it. This year, let us battle the hopelessness of infection, even as we mourn. Tisha B'Av is categorized as a *mo'ed*, a festival. It stands *Bein haMitzarim*, as the liminal person hovering on the boundary between one reality and another, between hope and despair, between acedia and a meaningful life.

Learning How to Cry

The author of this kinah echoes Yirmiyahu: "If only my head would be water and my eyes a spring of tears, so that I could cry all day and night for the slain of the daughter of my people" (Yirmiyahu 8:23). "If only someone would give me a traveler's lodge in the wilderness, then I would forsake my people and leave them, for they are all adulterers, a band of traitors" (9:1). He is frustrated by his tears' inability to express the full extent of his sorrow. He wants to escape the world and hide from the overwhelming nightmares of destruction and exile.

He echoes Iyov: "If only I knew how to find Him, I would approach His seat" (Iyov 23:3). "Pity me, pity me, O you, my friends, for the Hand of God has afflicted me! Why do you pursue me, as does God? If only my words would be written down! If only they would be inscribed in a book, with an iron stylus and lead engraved forever on rock!" (19:21–24). He, as Iyov, experiences Israel's rebuke from the other nations as a continuation of the destruction. The power of his words is thwarted by their fleeting meanings: Will others relate to all the pain and suffering embedded in his speech?

He echoes David HaMelech: "Then I said, 'O that I had a wing like the dove! I would fly off and find rest! Behold, I would wander afar. I would dwell in the wilderness" (Tehillim 55:7–8). The author of this lamentation wants to flee to where he can be with God, without the distraction and pain of his existence. And the author echoes God, as portrayed by Yeshayahu: "If only I were at war with the weeds and thorns (rather than Israel), I would then trample it and set it altogether on fire!"

This is why God responds to the lamentation: "From the moment Israel ceased to follow My ways, they abandoned Me, so I abandoned them. I grumbled and I groaned, my Innards and my Heart were spilled out in grief."

This kinah takes us through the intense process of crying, weeping, lamenting, screaming and agonizing over the destruction. Did anyone ever find the words to express the horrors of the Holocaust?

It then introduces the picture of God weeping with us and experiencing the same frustration over how to express the depth of His pain. Rabbi Nachman taught in the name of Shmuel, who taught in the name of Rabbi Yehoshua ben Korḥa, that the Holy One, Benedicted is He, summoned the ministering angels and asked them: "How does a flesh and blood king mourn?" The angels responded, "He drapes sackcloth over the entrances to his palace." God said, "So shall I do: I clothe the heavens in blackness and make sackcloth their garment!" (Yeshayahu 50:3).

But this was not sufficient. "How does a flesh and blood king mourn?" God asked again. "He dims the lights," came the angels' reply. And God said, "I shall do the same, as it is written, 'The sun and the moon have become blackened, and the stars have withdrawn their shine'" (Yoel 4:15).

Still, this was not enough. "How does a flesh and blood king mourn?" God asked again. "He overturns all the beds in the palace, so that no one sits normally," answered the angels. "I will do the same," said God. "I watched as thrones were set up, and the One of Ancient Days sat" (Daniel 7:9).

Still, this too was not enough. "How does a flesh and blood king mourn?" God asked again. "He walks barefoot," said the angels. Said God, "I will do the same. 'Clouds are the dust of His Feet'" (Naḥum 1:3).

Yet even then, God wanted another way to mourn. "How does a flesh and blood king mourn?" he asked, one last time. "He removes his royal robes," said the angels. "I will do the same," said God. He did as He planned and tore His garments (Eicha 2:17).

We are desperate to find tears, words, and mourning adequate to reflect the level of our pain. God is described in the midrash above and toward the end of this kinah as equally desperate to cry. This is remarkable as we recall that the first Tisha B'Av, in the desert after the sin of the spies, God criticized Israel for crying meaningless cries: "You have cried empty cries and I will give you real reasons to cry (Ta'anit 29a).

We do not cry because it is Tisha B'Av. Tisha B'Av is designed so that we will learn how to cry.

Reading the midrash, one might wonder why Hashem includes the angels in His mourning. They do not possess knowledge that He does not have; he designed the angels simply to carry out His Own Will. Why does Hashem ask the angels, beings of spirit, about the ways of the beings He Himself made of flesh and blood? And how do the angels know the ways of Man?

That we are here, I think, meant to see that, just as we are unsure how to adequately express our mourning, Hashem is teaching us to ask—that mourning is something we struggle to do together. That we are all in this together, us and Hashem and maybe even the angels. We all have a role to play, but more than that—we need to recognize each other for our mourning to have any meaning.

This Year!

"Every year, my people hope that this is the year of redemption."

—Ḥasam Sofer, Responsa

The Ḥasam Sofer wonders whether this is really a healthful approach to the diaspora. After all, how long can we keep on expecting this year to be the one?

In fact, we are declaring our belief that every year is filled with potential; we approach even the worst of times with expectation that things will become miraculously better.

I heard a story of an elderly Holocaust survivor who came to see Rav Chaim Shmuelevitz soon after being released from Auschwitz. The holy rabbi asked the man, "How did you survive?" The man looked at the Rabbi in total innocence and purity, and responded, "The Sanctification of the New Moon." The rabbi sat with his mouth open, "Whatever do you mean?"

The old man answered, "The benediction we recite says, 'To the moon He said that it should renew itself as a crown of splendor for those borne by Him from the womb, those who are destined to renew themselves like it, and to glorify their Molder for the name of His glorious kingdom.' How could I say these words and not believe that we were soon to be redeemed?"

We use this conviction that this will be the year of Redemption to survive anything and everything.

Swift as Eagles

"Would that I could soar to the sphere of the heaven."

This phrase is usually understood to be based on the verse from Yirmiyahu, "Behold, like an eagle the enemy will swoop down and spread its wings against Moav" (48:40).

Moav, an ancient enemy of Israel, was confident that they would defeat Israel and remain safe, because there were no indications that the Babylonians were planning to attack them, and they rejoiced at the vulnerability of Jerusalem. The prophet had a vision in which he saw the future great achievements of Nevuchadnetzar and the Babylonians (Vayikra Rabbah 13:5). He envisioned their armies swooping down on Moav, much as an eagle swoops down on its prey.

This vision of Babylon's great future is part of the idea that God will only allow a great nation to conquer Israel. God wants people to have the opportunity to understand that the success of the Babylonians, Persians, Greeks, and Romans against Israel was a gift from God. These nations were used as God's tools. The Babylonians' military successes were almost otherworldly. They were as swift as eagles. The author of this lamentation describes how he would need such miraculous assistance from God to be able to express the full extent of his grief over the destruction and exile.

In Sanhedrin 96b, the Talmud describes the scene of the Babylonians' successful breach of Jerusalem's walls as one in which the army had almost given up on successfully breaking into the holy city.

> *Rava said, "Nevuchadnetzar sent three hundred mules, laden with iron axes that cut iron, to Nevuzaradan. All of them were incapacitated at one gate of Jerusalem, as it reads, 'And now they hack its carved work together with hatchets and hammers' (Tehillim 74:6). Seeing this, he sought to return, saying, 'I am afraid.'*

> *"A Heavenly Voice said, 'Jumper, the son of a jumper, O Nevuzaradan, jump now, as the time has arrived for the Temple's destruction and the burning of the Sanctuary.' He still had one ax, and he struck the gate with, and it opened, as it reads, "He became known as one who lifts axes high against the thickets of forest' (Tehillim 74:5). Then he continued slaying everyone he encountered until he reached the Sanctuary and ignited a fire in it.*

> *"The Temple wanted to fly away, but Heaven tread it down, as it reads, 'God has trodden the virgin, the daughter of Yehudah, like a winepress' (Eicha 1:15).*

"Nevuzaradan became proud, and a Heavenly Voice said, 'You slew a slain nation, you burned a burnt temple, you ground up ground flour.'"

At the final moment, the walls miraculously fell without resistance, so that all would know that the Babylonians were simply God's tools.

Gittin 56a describes a similar situation during the Roman attack in Jerusalem:

The Emperor sent Nero the Caesar against them. As he was coming, he shot an arrow towards the east, and it fell in Jerusalem. He then shot one towards the west, and again it fell in Jerusalem. He shot towards all four directions of the Heavens, and each time it fell in Jerusalem. He said to a boy, "Repeat to me the last verse of Scripture you have learnt." The boy said, "And I will lay my vengeance upon Edom (Rome) by the hand of my people Israel" (Ezekiel 25:14). Nero said, "The Holy One, Benedicted be He, desires to lay waste his House and lay the blame on me." So he ran away and became a proselyte, and Rabbi Meir was descended from him.

Whomever the Nero described in the story was—we know that Nero never traveled to Jerusalem—he did not want to be God's agent of destruction, only to be punished.

The Kabbalists associate wings with *Din*, God's Attribute of Judgment. The eagle mentioned above does not fly, as *din* does not come from Above when expressed as destruction. It is the result of the destructive influences created by human beings on earth. Destructive judgment is not Divine. When people fail to take the proper precautions to keep each other safe, we cause our own suffering.

KINAH 9

Stirring the Dust

"How they have hurled My glorious crown from My Head."

On a certain island in the sea there lived a great sage, highly skilled in creating all manner of wonderful things. At first, the Sage lived alone on his island, content to enjoy his own thoughts. But this sage reflected that true wisdom demands that creatures be brought into existence to benefit from and enjoy that wisdom.

Consequently, he built a towering edifice, story upon story, with a closed, secret room at its summit, so cunningly concealed then no one but he could enter therein. Here in this room this Sage could enjoy his own thoughts, in lofty contemplation as he used to do before the great palace was erected. Beneath this room there were many walls and mansions endowed in miraculous fashion with intelligence so that they could appreciate the wisdom of the Sage, though they could not actually know him.

From time to time, the sage would emerge from his secret chamber to walk among the halls and mansions, endowing them with the power and intelligence to endure. As he passed through these rooms, the sage would come upon a spacious courtyard in which he had created birds of varied plumage, each with its own type of music and its own song. The Sage could observe these birds through the crystal walls of his palace, and their song would ascend to him, conducted by specially fashioned pipes.

Beneath this courtyard there was a garden containing water wheels. The wheels brought water to the flowers of the garden, where there were many more birds of a different feather. This garden contained many kinds of food and drink for the birds, and after drinking and eating their fill, they too would sing and their song would ascend to the Sage. But when this Sage was secluded in his room, he was indifferent to all that goes on beneath him, for the song of the birds was heard only in the halls and mansions, not in the secret chamber.

No sooner did the Sage leave his secret room to enter the lower rooms, than his power flew through them. He heard the song of the birds, which drew down through all the rooms to hear their sweet music. His presence gave the birds the strength to endure. These rooms, in turn, cast their light on the large courtyard to revive the birds. They caused the water wheels to function properly, bringing food and drink to the garden, so the birds could sing their song.

After singing for a time, the birds in the garden ascended by means of the water wheels to the large courtyard, where they were welcomed with great joy by the other birds because of the sweetness of their song. From here, they ascended to the halls and mansions, where the accents of their song swelled into joy, which the sage delighted to hear.

But the birds required great skill to sing the song as it should be sung. This scale could not be gained unless this sage, in his wisdom, taught it to the birds. The sage descended, therefore, into the garden, as soon as the birds were created, to teach them how to sing. For only when the melody was produced in its proper harmonies did it possess the power of penetrating to the upper rooms.

Yet it was not only lack of skill and ignorance of the melody that prevented the song from ascending. In the garden, there was a large quantity of a special dust, placed there to enable things to grow. This dust was valuable, and indeed essential, but if its placement on the ground was stirred and imbalanced, it rose to clog the channels through which the song of the birds ascended.

The birds had to be taught not only how to sing, but also how to avoid stirring up the dust by any frantic waving of their wings or by hopping about in forbidden territory. For when an inordinate amount of dust rose, it obscured the power-giving light from above and blocked the channels of song. This sage would then perforce remain in his secret chamber, oblivious to the birds, disturbing virtually the whole purpose for which he engaged in building.

In order to prevent the birds from stirring up the dust, this sage prepared pits at the bottom of the garden. Any bird failing to observe the rules, instead of ascending to the courtyard to sing its song there, was placed in one of these pits and covered with the dust it stirred. It was obliged to struggle there until it could escape from the dust and fly aloft to be welcomed with song. Some of the birds, having stirred up so much dust, would be suffocated beneath it forever and could never ascend to the upper rooms. Others, after having suffered in the dust, ultimately restored the proper balance and were then able to ascend (Shiur Komah 10).

Come to the Edge

Come to the edge.
We might fall.
Come to the edge.
It's too high!
COME TO THE EDGE!
And they came,
And he pushed,
And they flew.

—Christopher Logue

My wife and I were privileged this week to participate in a *Se'udat Hoda'ah*, a Thanksgiving Feast, offered by a family that had been pushed to the edge and experienced a great miracle. Their extended families and incredible friends held onto them for dear life and saved them from stepping over the precipice into hopelessness. Debbie and I were convinced that God was observing the gathering, deriving great nachas in the mutual love and support, faith and determination, of His children. On our way home, inspired by the event, I realized that the great miracle was not that the family was saved from falling over the edge, but that they had stepped over the edge, and rather than fall, they grew wings, and soared to unbelievable heights. I'm convinced that their miracle was God's response to their new wings.

My close friend who, battling his second bout with cancer was, with his family, pushed over the edge, but he did not fall; he flew. He didn't just survive; he grew wings. He is stronger, more attuned to life, perhaps even funnier than before.

Torah, as life, speaks differently to people who know how to fly: "Moshe began explaining the Torah five weeks before he died. The verse doesn't say that he continued his explanations of the past forty years, but that he began the explanation only now in his Final Lecture!" (Devarim 1:5).

Moshe could not have begun his explanation any earlier because the people had yet to grow *their* wings. As long as they had the greatest prophet in history, they could always turn to God for answers. They had the love of Aharon and the vision of Miriam. They were secure. Step by step, they were pushed to the edge. Miriam died. Aharon died. The generation that experienced Sinai was gone. The final push over the edge was the realization that Moshe would die and they would have to go on without him. The people were sad, but confident. They were frightened, but ready to move on. They grew wings. Now Moshe could begin explaining the Torah as it is—not as an instruction book for dealing with straightforward situations, but as a manual for people who want to grow wings and fly with independence. This moment was the real beginning of Torah.

The first Tisha B'Av was when the spies returned from Israel with a frightening report. The people cried, convinced that they were being pushed over the edge. They didn't have the courage to fly. The generation of the wingless died out and the new generation, ready to fly, received Moshe's new explanation of Torah. Only people who know how to fly can build the Land of Israel.

Each Tisha B'Av in history was followed by a new explanation of Torah: The exile to Babylon produced an Esther and eventually the Talmud. The destruction of the Second Temple led to the establishment of Yavneh as a center of learning. The destruction of European Jewry was followed by a generation of fliers who rebuilt Israel, struggling to incorporate all we have learned living on the edge during the Diaspora and the values that have kept us alive through the ages.

Yes, we've been pushed over the edge, time after time, but we always learned to fly. God says to Israel in the opening moments of Sinai, "That I have borne you on the wings of eagles," meaning, I trained you to fly; it is only when you grow your own wings that you will fully appreciate My gift of Torah (Shemot 19:4).

We sit on the ground on Tisha B'Av, just as mourners sit close to the earth from which they feel they have been pushed, but at midday, we rise with new wings, symbolized for men by the wings of the *tallit* worn only in the afternoon. It is as if to say, "We've been pushed over the edge, but we're ready to fly into the future." That, for me, is the most powerful moment of Tisha B'Av.

We have all been pushed to the edge this year. There are no guarantees of what awaits us, and we are at risk of plummeting into despair. Fear is always an opportunity for courage. We must do what we can to rise to the occasion— to hold our loved ones in our hearts, to save each other from hopelessness. It is time for us to fly.

The Murder of the Kohanim

"They drowned and slaughtered Kohanim and Levi'im who once maintained the tiers of my Temple platform. When, in the valley of Hamath, my Kohanim were murdered..."

The final phrase refers to II Melachim 25:18–21:

> *And the captain of the guard took Seraiah the chief Kohen, and Tzefanyah the second Kohen, and the three keepers of the door; and out of the city he took an officer that was set over the men of war; and five men of them that saw the king's face, who were found in the city; and the scribe of the captain of the host, who mustered the people of the land; and threescore men of the people of the land, that were found in the city. And Nevuzaradan, the captain of the guard, took them and brought them to the king of Babylon to Rivlah. And the king of Babylon smote them, and put them to death at Rivlah in the land of Ḥamat. So Yehudah was carried away captive out of his land.*

The Beit HaMikdash was destroyed. Jerusalem was in ruins. The king was executed. These verses describe the execution of the Kohen Gadol. Few biblical scenes are more devastating. What do the Sages learn from these verses?

There is a discussion in the Talmud about the number of people called up to the Torah on different holidays. What is the significance of three, five, and seven? Different answers were given by Rav Yitzhak ben Nahmani and Rav Shimon ben Pazi, or, according to others, Rav Shimon ben Pazi and Rav Yitzhak ben Nahmani, or according to others, Rav Shmuel ben Nahmani alone.

One said that the number of people called up to the Torah represents the respective number of Hebrew words in the verses of the priestly benedictions. The other said that three people correspond to the murdered Kohanim in Babylon. Rav Yosef learnt, "Three, five and seven: 'three keepers of the door,' five of them that saw the king's face,' and 'seven that saw the king's face.'"

The Talmud finds a source for halacha even in this devastating scene. It's worthwhile to pause and take stock at this point and reflect on the powerful message the Sages are teaching: Find meaning even in horrible experiences.

This is one of the strengths that has maintained us through the millennia of exile. When we grapple with horrible experiences of past or present, we should try to take a moment to find some meaning in it. We should find ways to memorialize the lives that we have lost.

KINAH 10

The Rose of Sharon

O how the Rose of Sharon sits alone and joy has been silenced from the mouths of those who carried the Ark; And the Kohanim, the sons of Aharon, were removed from their watches.

"I am the Rose of Sharon, a lily of the valleys." The Community of Israel said, "I am the one, and beloved ('ḥavivah,' as in 'havatzelet') am I. I am she whom the Holy One, Benedicted is He, loved more than the seventy nations. 'A Rose of Sharon,' so called because I made Him a shade ('tzeil') by the hand of Betzalel, as it is written, 'And Betzalel made the ark' (Shemot 37:1). 'Of Sharon,' so called because I chanted to Him a song ('shirah') together with Moshe, as it is written, 'Then sang Moshe and the Children of Israel' (Shemot 15:1)."

—Shir Hashirim Rabbah II:I

This kinah takes all three stages of this midrash to remark on how the Rose of Sharon has fallen. I am she whom the Holy One, Benedicted is He, loved more than the seventy nations, but now, I the beloved sit alone. I made Him a shade, the Ark, but now joy has been silenced from the mouths of those who carried the Ark. I chanted a song, but now my joy has been silenced, and I weep (Shir Hashirim Rabbah II.I).

We contrast how our tragic state from what we know we are in our essence, lamenting that we are unable to live as our true selves. We still aspire to be God's beloved, the ones who create a place for Him, the ones who sing His song. But we must recapture our essence before we can be the Rose of Sharon once more.

The midrash continues:

> *Another explanation: "I am the Rose of Sharon," I am the one, and beloved am I. I am she who was hidden ("ḥavuyah") in the shadow ("b'tzeil") of Egypt, and in a brief space the Holy One, Benedicted is He, brought me to Ramses, and I blossomed forth in good deeds like a rose, and I chanted before Him the song, as it says, "You shall have a song in the night when a feast is hallowed" (Yeshayahu 30:29).*

We were hidden in the shadow of Egypt, waiting for the opportunity to blossom and sing. We are now hidden in exile, again waiting to bloom and sing in joy.

All this serves as the introduction to a kinah that focuses on the twenty-four Priestly Watches and the cities in which they were based.

The Kohanim used to serve in the Temple for one week and then return home. Each of our twenty-four regions had regular reminders of people preparing and sanctifying themselves to serve in Jerusalem. The Kohanim returned with tales and lessons of the Beit HaMikdash, and for everyone in those areas, this served as an established part of their lives. That connection with the Beit HaMikdash was a constant reminder that we are the Rose of Sharon.

The Coronavirus pandemic exiled us even further, confining us to our homes, disrupting our established routines, disconnecting us from our usual sense of togetherness. We are hidden in our exiles, waiting to return. And what will we bring with us when we do? The tales and lessons from our communities—from all of us. As alone and separate as we may feel, we are still in this together. And just as we share each other's pain, the time will come when we can unite and share in each other's joy.

Joy as a *Tikkun*

My enemies heard that I was stained
And that my prayers were shut out;
He gave me neither mercy or pity.
Gone from Kiryat Ḥanah was
The watch residing in Kefar Yoḥana.

This kinah turns our attention from the destruction of the Temple to the loss of the priestly families. The Zohar equates the loss of the Kohanim to the loss of joy in our Service of God. Rabbi Yehudah opens his lecture with, "Serve Hashem with joy" (Tehillim 100:2). We learn that a person's service of God must be performed with joy and zest, so that it will be whole.

How is this possible in the case of an offering, which is brought in teshuvah for violating one of God's commandments? With what face can such a person stand before God? Surely, only with a contrite spirit and sorrowful heart. Where, then, is the joy and celebration?

The joy and celebration were delivered by the Kohanim and Levi'im. The Kohen rejoiced because he was far from chastisement and could show a merrier face than the rest of the people. The Levi'im provided the music. The Kohen stood by the repentant person and found suitable words to joyfully unify the Holy Name, while the Levi'im sang.

At the present day, there are no offerings. If a person sins and returns to the Master with bitterness of heart, with sorrow, with weeping and contrition, how is he to provide joy and singing?

We have learned, "A person should enter the synagogue to the extent of Two Gateways and then pray" (Midrash Tehillim 24:7). This alludes to the words of David HaMelech, "Lift up your heads, O you gates" (Tehillim 24:7). A person should focus his mind on the Holy of Holies, which represents the Holy Name, before he recites his prayer. The first joy is the Community of Israel, and Israel will one day come forth from exile through this joy, as it is written, "For in joy you will go forth" (Yeshayahu 55:12). When the person realizes this, he will increase his joy, thus the second gate, and will express it in song (Zohar, III 8b).

A *tikkun* for this kinah is to approach God with joy and celebration. When we experience any joy in our service, recognize that this joy is the key to redemption. This should thereby increase our joy to the point that we are celebrating joy itself!

These days, many of us find it hard to be joyful (including Kohanim and Levi'im). But there are those among us who inspire us with their optimism and good spirits. Such people can provide joy for the rest of us, even when we cannot personally access those feelings amidst our own sadness. And nobody should feel pressured to be that joyous person all the time. We can take it in turns, allowing ourselves to process whatever we authentically feel. There will always be someone to feel that happiness and hope, someone who can bring us song.

True Wealth

In the 1500s and 1600s, two countries seemed to defy all that had gone before. Spain amassed the largest supply of gold in history thanks to its New World conquests, but saw inflation and near bankruptcy as a result. In Holland, the Dutch were gaining greater wealth than almost any country on earth by trading in fish and other mundane items, in the beginnings of a strange new way that came to be known as a market economy, as described by Joyce Appleby in *The Relentless Revolution*:

> *During the seventeenth century, the Dutch extracted tons of herring from waters that washed on English shores, had the largest merchant fleet in Europe, drew into their banks Spanish gold, borrowed at the lowest interest rates, and bested all comers, in the commerce of the Baltic, the Mediterranean, and the West Indies. Dutch prosperity, like Dutch land, seemed to have been created out of nothing. The inevitable contrast with Spain, the possessor of gold and silver mines now teetering on the verge of bankruptcy, only underscored the conundrum of Dutch success.*

The midrash on Eichah is filled with fantastic tales of the greatness that was Jerusalem's before the destruction of the Second Temple. Although there are numerous stories describing people's great material wealth, there are far more tales of the incredible brain power in Jerusalem. They are tales of a different form of wealth. They are tales of a people with absolutely everything they needed to succeed and thrive, and yet they failed, disastrously so.

These midrashim are the stories of creative people, entrepreneurs, who expended effort after effort only to fail. They are the story of gifted people who did not know how to manage failure. They lost faith in their gifts. They did not appreciate their unusual form of wealth. They were exiles long before they were exiled. They lost their connection with their gifts. They lost their connection with themselves.

Theirs are the story of the student who struggles with Talmud and does not apply himself to other areas of study. He does not become a *talmid ḥacham* and never experiences the joy of Torah. He may possess numerous gifts, but he desires the one that all others honor; he desires the Spanish gold, rather than enjoying his own treasures.

Theirs are the stories of the people who pray every day and work hard to fulfill all the mitzvot, but feel empty in their observance. They want to pray with the same passion and insight as the great rabbis and *tzaddikim*, and when they cannot, mistake themselves for spiritual paupers. Rather than fixating on Spanish gold, they should amass their own wealth by identifying their own strengths.

We don't need everyone to be good at the same things to become great as a whole. It is through our different strengths that we can strengthen each other. Now, when we are confined to our separate spaces, we have the golden opportunity to reflect on our own gifts. We should each reevaluate our individual selves to see how we are best equipped to serve our communities. Once we connect with ourselves, we are better able to connect with each other, and share our wealth.

KINAH 11

A Measure of Righteousness

The Egyptians and the Assyrians were battling for supremacy. Jerusalem, in the midst of a spiritual renaissance under King Yoshiyahu, stood between them. The Egyptians, unconcerned with militarily insignificant Yehudah, asked to pass peacefully through the area to battle the Assyrians. But Yoshiyahu refused to grant them permission, having studied Parshat Beḥukotai: "And I will give peace in the land, and you shall lie down, and none shall make you afraid; and I will cause evil beasts to cease out of the land, neither shall the sword go through your land" (Vayikra 26:6).

The king was justifiably proud of leading Bnei Yisrael back to God as no one in history had done before. He was confident that his nation was righteous in God's Eyes and merited the promise that "no sword shall pass through your land." Surely God would keep His word and protect them from even an Egyptian sword passing through their land. Yirmiyahu warned the king not to involve Jerusalem in this battle. Yet Yoshiyahu, confident in his people's righteousness, stormed south to stop the Egyptians—only to be killed in the ensuing battle.

How odd that a man convinced that no sword shall pass through the land would lift his sword to stop the Egyptians! How odd that a man so confident in his nation's righteousness would ignore the warnings of a prophet! How sad that a man could be so blinded by his righteousness.

I recall the Friday night meal immediately after the Six Day War, when all had witnessed numerous miracles, none more powerful than the reunification of Jerusalem. The family members and many students who sat at our table were in a celebratory mood. They were critical of those who credited Israel's military strength, rather than God, when I asked what most considered a 'mood killer' question: "Why did God make this happen? Did we do something to deserve it?"

"Anyone who believes that we deserved this miracle because of our righteousness is making the same mistake as Yoshiyahu," my father, *zt"l*, answered. "The people who fought and risked their lives earned the miracles."

"Is that righteousness?" I asked. "Yoshiyahu risked his life to fight. Why was he not granted the same miracles?"

"Someone who fights, convinced of his righteousness, is just as bad, if not worse, than one who credits his military strategy and power. Beware of people who are convinced that they are righteous!"

According to the *haftarah* for Beḥukotai, "Cursed is the man who trusts in man, and whose heart departs from Hashem" (Yirmiyahu 17:5). Perhaps this alludes, not only to those who trust in their military might, but to those who trust in their own righteousness.

There is another danger when we are surrounded by people who proclaim their own righteousness: far too many become convinced of their "sinfulness"—that they are undeserving of God's miracles, that He would not listen to their prayers, let alone help them. The inevitable result is that "their hearts depart from Hashem." Their hearts can depart from their people, too, amongst whom they may feel unworthy. Perhaps saddest of all, if they do not trust in their own merit, their hearts might even depart from themselves.

I've met many people who authoritatively stated that my grandfather and father were insufficiently righteous. I've met far more people who believe they are unworthy. I have yet to find a righteousness thermometer. My favorite interactions are with those who "Walk in My Statutes," measuring themselves by how well they follow the path of halacha, the path of "walkers." I admire those who look only to their own feet, committed to always walk forward, one step at a time.

In these devastating times, it is dangerously easy to authoritatively declare that we are being Divinely punished. We have not caused a global pandemic with our "sins." And no one, absolutely no one, is beyond redemption. There is no guarantee of personal survival; we cannot rely on miracles. But we can ask for them and we can take steps to make them. Hashem listens to all of us. Keep praying. Keep fighting. Keep walking. We can all be righteous, and we can all be mighty, and we can all do our part to protect our shared life on *Olam HaZeh*.

KINAH 12

My Tent

"My tent that You yearned, even before Creation, to align with Your celestial Throne of Glory, why is it forever plundered by the hands of the plunderers?"

Each stanza of this kinah begins with "My Tent," alluding to the Mishkan and the Beit HaMikdash. This concept developed from Eichah: "He bent his bow like an enemy. His right hand poised like a foe, He slew all who were of pleasant appearance. In the Tent of the Daughter of Zion, He poured out His wrath like fire" (2:4).

Rabbi Avraham Galanti suggests that we imagine the world as the inside of a tent (*Kol Bochim*). The cover is the Presence of God, hovering above to protect and nurture all that lies within. The tent itself is magnificent, shining its light inside, so that everything reflects the glory of the tent itself.

We find the first allusion to this idea in the opening verses of the Torah: "And the Divine Presence hovered upon the surface of the waters" (Bereishit 1:2). Rashi comments, "The Divine Throne floated in the air and hovered over the water with the *ruaḥ*, wind, from God's Mouth, and His Word, like a dove that hovers over her nest." The creation of the world began with Hashem "Tenting" over the earth. He protected His creation as a mother bird hovers over her nest of eggs.

Hashem used a similar process to create Adam: "A mist ascended from the earth and watered the whole surface of the soil. And Hashem, God, formed the man of dust from the ground, and He blew into his nostrils the soul of life; and the man became a living being" (Bereishit 2:6–7). The Talmud perceives that mist as a tent, so much so that it derives the laws of the sukkah from the verse. The mist formed the tent and nurtured life within.

The Mishkan and Beit HaMikdash were miniature creations of the world and Man. The Mishkan's coverings and the Temple's roof represented God's hovering Presence over His creation. This is why we have so many powerful descriptions of the Beit HaMikdash as "My Tent" in this kinah—"My Tent that You yearned before Creation," "My Tent that You guided with clouds of splendor," "My Tent that You positioned as a foundation," and so forth.

"My Tent" is an awesome symbol of God's active involvement in Creation. When God destroyed it, we wonder about His continued role in our lives. We who knew the shelter of His Presence are lost in the "open skies" of this world. The kinah ends thus:

> *After and before, both this time and that,*
> *in each and every generation, God's anger*
> *and protective shelter are made known.*
> *So why, of all nations, has He pressed His*
> *   Hand upon me?*

This is evident, although my destruction is
engraved upon His Palm,
nevertheless, my healing is certain,
for His anger is but for a moment.
Still, I wonder, how has He clouded
me until now in His anger?

We can find God's shelter "in each and every generation."
Even now, when the world outside is a danger to us, we may
find it in the safety our homes. But as long as He clouds me
in His anger, I will wonder: Where is my Tent?

KINAH 13

Just So

This Kinah is uses the phrase "*Ei Ko*" as a play on the word "*Eichah.*" Where is the *ko*, the "so," in "so said God?"

When God uses the term *ko*, He demonstrates an intense degree of *Hashgacha Pratit*, Divine Providence, and reveals manifest love for Israel.

Therein lies the problem. Most of us are confused by the system of *hashgacha*. Many of us believe that everything is *ko*, exact, just so. We are confused when things don't make sense. We wonder, "Where is *ko*? Where is a world that works just so?"

Rabbeinu Yonah describes Israel as challenging God: "We do not experience You as compassionate, but cruel. We do not see justice, but suffering. You must restore justice to the world before we can return to You" (Berachot 19b in the Rif). Rabbeinu Yonah is describing a cry of "*Ei Ko.*"

We are confused by the lack of *ko* in the world. We are confused by the absence of *ko* in the teachings of our leaders, who do not agree on basic concepts of *hashkafa*, Jewish philosophy. This is particularly true now. The world is in a state of disorder. We do not know if we can trust our leadership, or which leaders to trust, and our very lives are on the line. The prophet, Yirmiyahu, cries out to us, "*Eichah*!" We respond, "*Ei Ko?*"

The Oakling & the Oak

This Tisha B'Av kinah bemoans the seeming loss of the Divine promises to the Patriarchs. We have a strange relationship with the Patriarchs, on whom we depend for the merit to protect us and defend us before God. And yet... how can we ever measure up to them?

Hartley Coleridge, son of the famous Romantic poet Samuel Taylor Coleridge, only published one volume of poetry in his lifetime. An 1833 review praised his verse for embodying "no trivial inheritance of his father's genius," but also quoted the old saying that "the oakling withers beneath the shadow of the oak."

Jean-Paul Sartre counted himself lucky that he was an infant when his father died. He wrote, "Had my father lived, he would have lain on me at full length and crushed me" (*Les Mots*). Those are harsh words. But it's true that parents can be "crushing"—particularly fathers, and particularly with eldest sons. (I urge you to read *The Oakling and The Oak*, by my favorite essayist Anne Fadiman, and *Einstein's Dream's,* by physicist Alan Lightman. Both pose the question of how we could achieve anything if our ancestors lived in their full capacities forever.)

Is it possible that part of what led to the Temple's destruction was the loss of our wholehearted connection with our Patriarchs, ancestors, parents, and teachers? Is it possible that we were so desperate to make our mark on the world that we severed important connections to our past?

If we desire to reconnect to the Divine promises made to the Patriarchs, perhaps the first step is reconnecting to the Patriarchs themselves. As we look to towards rebuilding our communities, let us remember the Patriarchs. Did we appeal to them when we asked Hashem for protection? What can *we* do to protect *their* legacy?

Script or Writer

Remember what Chardin told us at the Salon:

Gentlemen, gentlemen, be lenient. Look through all the paintings here and find the worst, and know that two thousand poor devils have bitten their brushes to pieces in despair of ever doing as badly. You all call Parrocel a dauber, and so he is, if you compare him with Verner, but he's a rare talent compared with the multitude of those who've abandoned the career they entered with him.

Le Mayne used to say that it took thirty years' practice to be able to turn one's original sketch into a painting, and Le Mayne was no fool. If you'll listen to what I say, perhaps you'll learn to be indulgent.

—Denis Diderot, *The Salons*

In this kinah, we ask God, "Where is the promise You made to Avraham, Yitzḥak, and Yaakov?" I can hear the unspoken challenge to this question: "Who are you to compare yourselves to the Patriarchs? Are you not the ones who forfeit the connection to their merit? (See Kinah 26, "As Parents for Children.")

In "The Oakling & the Oak," we began discussing the challenge of living with great parents, and the dangers of comparing ourselves to them. In Kinah 4's "The Hovering Life," we wondered about the impact of the competition between Samaria and Jerusalem had on both populations. Diderot's report reminds us to be patient when judging good artists who fail to match the great ones. How are we to ask, "Where is Your promise to the Patriarchs in our lives? Where was it at each stage of our suffering?" Are we, as Chardin advises, asking God to indulge us and be lenient? Or are we asking for the same promise He made Avraham?

In Kinah 7's "Above the Stars," we explained God's promise to Avraham as giving his descendants the means to raise themselves into a reality of their own making. The words *koh yi'hyeh zar'acha* mean, "Your children will be *koh,* just like you, and have the ability to rise above their destiny and create new destinies for themselves." We are asking, "Where is that promise?" Perhaps we are not asking God, but rather, for ourselves: Are we even striving to live above the stars and create new destinies?

This kinah is the reverse image of Kinah 3, which describes people limited by an imposed destiny—people who cease to use their Free Choice. This is a natural consequence of destruction and exile. Are we following a prewritten script, or are we scriptwriters? Are we stuck where we were in Kinah 3, or have we accepted the challenge of living as *koh*—as Avrahams who write our own script and change the world?

Our post-pandemic life has not been prescribed for us. We are the writers. Let's change our world together.

KINAH 14

As Adam

"He cut down to size the great height of the man He fashioned."

As God placed Adam into the Garden of Eden, He took him from tree to tree, pointing out the beauty and benedictions of each creation. God instructed Adam to work the garden and care for everything that grew there.

This is exactly the point of Torah and mitzvot. Each mitzvah is a way to nurture God's garden. Each time we study Torah, we are nurturing the garden and learning how to care for everything in Creation. A person who studies Torah and performs mitzvot as a gardener will find that he changes his environment. People will be drawn to him as they perceive that he is making the entire area grow and flourish.

This must be our intention each time we study Torah and with each mitzvah that we perform: We are working in God's garden, nurturing it, making it more beautiful, and creating an environment in which His Presence is manifest.

Right now, our environments are smaller, almost as if we have our own private gardens. Yet every one of us still has the opportunity to care for Creation. One who lives alone can nurture himself or herself, and indeed, we should all make sure to do so. Those with others in their households can nurture the people around them. And thanks to technology, we are able to inspire countless people from a distance. We are all still tending God's garden, flourishing as best we can and helping each other grow.

Our global environment needs tending, too. Even before the Coronavirus pandemic, the world has been plagued by natural tragedies. This year alone, we have locusts in East Africa, wildfires in Australia, the highest ever rate of deforestation in the still-burning Amazon rainforest... Even under our current conditions, there are steps that we can take to help. We can limit our plastic and disposable products to reduce our carbon footprint. We can do our billing electronically to minimize paper waste. If our health permits, we can use fewer cooling and heating services to be more energy efficient. Our choices have a tangible impact, not only here, but on other countries whose resources we utilize.

Of course, it is hard for us as individuals to protect the entire world. Much of that responsibility rests on our leadership. However, it is our responsibility as individuals to choose, empower, and work with our leaders. Hashem entrusted *all* of us with His Creation. Let us each make the changes of which we are capable and guard His wonders together.

The Spectator & the Agent

*"When I endeavor to examine my own
conduct, I divide myself as it were into two
persons; and that I, the examiner and the
judge, represent a different character from
the other I, the person whose conduct is
examined into and judged of. The first is the
spectator. The second is the agent, a person
who I properly call myself, and on whose
conduct I was endeavoring to form some
opinion."*

—Adam Smith, *The Theory of Modern
Sentiments*

When I first read the comments of this eighteenth-century
philosopher, I focused on the importance of accepting the
role of Spectator. Then I came across this quote again in an
old notebook and read it differently. Although most of us fail
as the Spectator, the more significant failure is our denial of
the role of what Smith called the Agent.

The Sages of the Talmud and Midrash can find so many
causes for the destruction of the Temple. How, then, did the
generation of the destruction fail to notice their
wrongdoings? How did they fail to recognize the
consequences of their actions, when so many of prophets
warned them of the coming cataclysm? Even after the fact,

they failed to acknowledge that they caused their own destruction. They refused to accept that they were active Agents in the grand movements of history all around them. A person who rejects his role as an Agent can never become the Spectator, the examiner and judge of his conduct.

As we discussed in Kinah 13's "Just So," the midrash discovers that the earliest allusion to Tisha B'Av in God's "question" to Adam: *Ayeka* ("Where are you?") can also be read as *Eichah*.

Adam was hiding. Rather than emerge from his hiding place among the Garden's trees and say, "I ate of the tree You prohibited to me and realized that I am naked," Adam hid. He was passive. He did not see himself as an Agent who could repair, or at the very least address, his transgression. By rejecting the role of Agent, he forfeited the role of Spectator. He could not judge himself if he did not recognize his own ability to act on that judgment.

Adam failed his one test and no longer believed that his actions could make a difference. His destruction began, not with his "sin," but with his sense of inadequacy. He shed his agency and hid, to ashamed to even look at himself.

Perhaps the failure of the generations of the First and Second Temples was not their refusal to be Spectators and evaluate their behavior. Perhaps it was their fear of accepting themselves as Agents, active participants in all the terrible events around them.

How often do we view ourselves as victims of the anger of other people? Most of the people with whom I speak on this subject begin with how unreasonable a spouse or friend can be. There are also the people who immediately accept that God is punishing them when something bad happens. They cross the street without looking, are almost hit by a car, and declare, "God was punishing me for arguing with my parents!" It is as if we are all victims and none of us Agents. No wonder we have so much difficulty becoming the Spectator who can judge his own actions!

I fear that if we approach Tisha B'Av as a long list of our sufferings over the millennia of exile, we will continue to see ourselves as victims rather than Agents. If we do not accept our agency, we can never become Spectators. Our approach to Tisha B'Av must be that of Agents, accepting that we play important roles in life and in the world.

We must search for ways to actively rebuild all that has been destroyed. It is not enough to say, "I will not sin during the Three Weeks," for that is not the statement of an Agent. The Agent is active. The Agent asks, "What can I do to change my life and the world?" Only Agents can become Spectators and evaluate themselves during the period of teshuvah that soon follows Tisha B'Av.

We are not meant to blame ourselves for the pandemic itself. However, we *are* meant to ensure that we do not prolong it by acting irresponsibly. Are we socially distancing? Are we wearing masks if we need to leave the house? Are we taking care of ourselves and being mindful of our health?

Are we so eager to rebuild that we reopen too soon? There is so much work to be done. We must wield our Agency through the discerning eyes of the Spectator, proceeding with caution and with wisdom.

KINAH 15

The Poison Squad

On Prussic acid we break our fast;
 we lunch on a morphine stew;

We dine with a match-head consommé;
 drink carbolic acid brew;

...Thus all the "deadlies" we double-dare
 to put us beneath the sod;

We're death-immunes and we're proud as
proud—
 Hooray for the Pizen Squad!

— S.W. Gillilan, "The Song of the Poison Squad"

A menu for a 1902 holiday dinner had a healthy serving of Borax—yes, the poison—after the applesauce, after the soup, after the turkey, after the vegetables, and a final serving after dessert.

In "Death in the Pot," Deborah Blum describes the horrifying discoveries of Dr. Harvey Washington Wiley, a chemist from the US Department of Agriculture. "He suspected that the country was suffering from coast-to-coast poisoning, strictly due to commercial food production," she explains. He assembled a team to test preservatives and additives to processed foods, earning the moniker "The Poison Squad." Their horrific findings drew much public attention and influenced popular culture, including the above poem by S.W. Gillilan.

This kinah describes how we continue to drink a Poison Stew, the Golden Calf Consommé: "He remembers my circling the Golden Calf in the desert heat. He insists that He will never forget even as the shadows of evening grow long, 'I will bring a sword against you.'"

In Sanhedrin 102a, Rav Oshiya and Rav Yitzḥak provide two explanations of this: Rav Oshiya said, "Until Jeroboam, Israel imbibed a sinful disposition from one calf; but from him onwards, from two or three calves." His understanding is that we drink from the negative power of our transgressions. Rav Yitzchak said, "No retribution whatsoever comes upon the world which does not contain a slight fraction of the first calf, as it is written, 'Nevertheless in the day when I visit, I will visit their sin upon them' (Shemot 32:34)." According to this interpretation, we sip the consequences of our transgressions.

The kinah author finds an allusion to the Golden Calf in the Revelation at Sinai: "I will bring a sword against you." One of the primary laws of the *Mizbei'aḥ* is, "And if you make for me an altar of stone, you shalt not build it of hewn stones; for if you wave your sword upon it, you will have profaned it" (Shemot 20:21). This evokes the expulsion from Eden: "So He drove out the man; and He placed at the east of the garden of Eden the cherubim, and the flaming sword which turned every way, to guard the way to the Tree of Life" (Bereishit 3:24).

This phrase, "east of the garden of Eden," is referenced in the penultimate verse of Eichah: "Bring us back to You, Hashem, and we shall return, renew our days as of old." *K'kedem,* "as of old," can also be read "as of east," meaning East of Eden. After Adam was expelled, he had only to battle the flaming sword to regain access to the Garden, eat of the Tree of Knowledge, and become immortal—but he never did. We want to have the same access to the boundaries of Eden, so that we can demonstrate our willingness to fight that sword.

The poison we are drinking predates the Golden Calf and goes all the way back to Adam. It is the poison of fear that blocks us from achieving our potential.

We find ourselves now in a climate of fear. That fear is not misguided; in fact, it often demonstrates wisdom. We must, of course, strictly abide by the restrictions in place to keep us safe. The way to fight our "sword" is, ironically, by remaining where we are and biding our time. Yet some of our fears can endanger us. For example, we must not let fear stop us from taking these safety measures.

But we may also be afraid of what awaits us when this period of lives has ended. How can we return to normalcy? What should our communal life be like? This is where our true potential lies—in bravely taking steps to creating and renewing our Yiddishkeit. This is our path to the East of Eden.

Can You Hear Me?

*"I instructed your judges at that time, saying,
'Listen among your brethren.'"*

—Devarim 1:16

One of the major themes in Sefer Devarim is the relationship between seeing and hearing. "Hearing cannot compare to seeing," the Talmud insists, but we still must ask which comes first. We cannot see until we can hear.

The first quality of a judge must be his ability to listen. Shlomo HaMelech took Moshe's lesson to heart when Hashem appeared to him in a dream. "Request what I should give you," said Hashem. The young king replied, "May You grant Your servant a heart that can hear" (I Kings 3:5).

Shlomo did not need the fifth and final book of the Torah to know that he needed the gift of hearing. He needed only to look to Bnei Yisrael's experience at Har Sinai. Hashem offered us His covenant three times before Israel famously responded, "*Na'aseh v'nishma,* we will do and we will hear" (Shemot 24:7). Hashem had waited for this promise, wrapping Himself in cloud—an image that should be familiar to us from our discussion in "The Futility in Our Words." Yet here, we are given a very different understanding of its significance.

"I come to you in the thickness of the cloud," Hashem told Moshe, "so that the people will hear as I speak to you" (Shemot 19:9). Unlike the cloud that stopped Hashem from hearing our prayers, this was a cloud to help *us* hear *Hashem*.

The Israelites needed to hear before they could see "the thunder and the flames, the sound of the shofar" (Shemot 20:15). Their sight became so powerful that they could even see *sound.* But before they unlocked this unfathomable power of sight, they needed to learn hearing, as would our judges, and as would Shlomo.

No wonder the Haftarah of *Ḥazon*, Vision, begins with, "Hear, O Heavens, and give ear, O Earth" (Yeshayahu 1:2). The people had to learn how to hear before they could share Yeshayahu's vision. This is why we must hear our own words when we pray the "silent" Amidah. This is why the Shema is so essential to our faith. Our ability to hear is the first key to rebuilding all that was destroyed on Tisha B'Av.

Adam was not condemned to die immediately after his transgression. He first had a chance to repair the damage: "They heard the sound of Hashem, God, walking in the Garden toward evening, and the man and his wife hid from Hashem, God, among the trees of the Garden" (Bereishit 3:8). They had transgressed, yet they were still able to hear God's Voice traveling through the Garden. They still retained a hint of all their power and potential. Adam and Ḥavah could have stood up, faced God, repaired the damage, and lived forever. It was only when they ignored the Voice of God saying, "Where are you? *Eichah!*" that Death came (see Kinah 14, "The Spectator & the Agent"). It was only when they ignored their ability to hear that they acted as mere mortals.

When Yeshayahu spoke to Israel, the people had an opportunity to hear the Voice of God: "If you will be willing and you will hear, you shall eat the goodness of the land" (Yeshayahu 1:19). When they did not acknowledge their ability to hear, Yeshayahu responded, *"Eichah!"* (Yeshayahu 1:21).

When Yirmiyahu spoke, Israel had the opportunity to hear the Voice of God again. They, like Adam, could have faced up to their mistakes and repaired the damage. They were still able to hear, yet they refused to listen. They did not *want* to listen. They could not acknowledge their own greatness in the face of their many failures. They shut their ears, and Yirmiyahu cried, *"Eichah!"*

We may not hear with the same sensitivity as Adam or the legendary wisdom of Shlomo. We do not have Yeshayahu and Yirmiyahu speaking to us in the Voice of God. But we, the nation of Shema, can hear God's Voice in His Torah and mitzvot. We must "listen among our brethren"—to each other, to ourselves, to the Divine spark within us all. Only when we learn to hear can we merit seeing our redemption.

Do we let the Heavens cloud our voices from Hashem? Or do we, O Israel, cloud our eyes with our hands and hear His Voice call out to us? This year, we have witnessed and experienced undeniable threats to our national and global communities, be they the pandemic, racial violence, or environmental devastation. These extraordinarily painful circumstances are, like everything else, calls for personal growth and communal change. Are we listening?

KINAH 16

Absent the Light

In your light I learn how to love.
In your beauty, how to make poems.
You dance inside my chest, where no one sees you,
but sometimes I do,
and that sight becomes this art.

—Rumi, 1235

Remember what the foe, Titus, did within the Temple
  precincts.
He drew forth his sword and entered the Holy of Holies.
He shocked our heritage when he profaned the Show Bread
and pierced the curtain, embroidered on both sides.

Our enemies would say that if Titus could do as he did, there was nothing in the Holy of Holies. We say that Titus was unable to see the light and the beauty within.

We can still say to God, "You dance inside my chest, where no one sees You." Our enemies would say that there is nothing dancing inside our chests, that the dance is imaginary. They would say that our tears today are empty.

We respond by transforming our tears into art. We study the messages of all the calamities of Tisha B'Av, applying lessons to our lives and striving to nurture a relationship with God. This is an Art. We can do the same with the calamities of today, learning and nurturing and painting our Yiddishkeit with the light and beauty of our hearts.

Remember!

"In the seventh year of Yehu, Yeho'ash became king, and he reigned in Jerusalem forty years. His mother's name was Tziviah; she was from Be'ersheva. Yoash did what was right in the eyes of God all the years Yehoyada the Kohen instructed him. The high places, however, were not removed; the people continued to offer sacrifices and burn incense there."

—II Melachim 12:2-3

The world was shocked and horrified when confronted by images of concentration camps. General Eisenhower insisted that the scenes be recorded for posterity. No one could deny the Holocaust.

This was the first time that the world understood the suffering of the Jewish people. No one was horrified by the Babylonian massacres. There were no films of the horrors perpetrated by the Romans. The world was silent after the Crusades. No one other than the people of Israel cried over the countless pogroms, expulsions, and blood libels. We needed to cry, "Remember!" No one else gave our suffering any thought. No one was horrified. The Holocaust was different. The world joined us in, "Remember!"

120

No more. Governments massacre their citizens and no one yells in outrage. Israel defends itself and the world condemns us. It seems that they have forgotten. It is no longer *verboten* to deny the Holocaust. We find the cries of "Remember!" to be our own. People are not listening.

Our remembrance is not shared. When others demanded "Remember!" alongside us, we began to rely on them. We wanted them to believe us; we had never experienced the world's sympathy. We were desperate for validation and empathy—so desperate that even now, we flounder as the world turns against us. The voices of denial are drowning us out, and the cry of "Remember!" is only ours once more.

When we cry for remembrance, we recall not only tragedy, but our successes and greatness. When we remember for our own sake, we draw on our inner strength. We fight for our survival, not the world's approbation. This kinah of "Remember!" is ours, and ours alone.

KINAH 18

Beyond Room

I just read *Room*, by Emma Donoghue, and haven't been able to stop thinking about what happens when Room opens. Room, totally enclosed except for a tiny skylight, is the entire world of Jack, a five-year-old prisoner who lives in Room with Ma. He and Ma use their imaginations to fill their days. Room has everything Jack needs and desires—until Ma, who has been imprisoned for seven years, wants more for her son and plans their escape.

I cheered for Jack as he helps Ma with their daring rescue. I was so focused on his chance to experience Outside that I wasn't prepared for how frightening and difficult it would be for him to adjust to life beyond Room. At the end of the book, Jack insists that Ma take him back. Yet when they see the storage shed that was Room, Jack struggles to accept that it is the same place: "We step in through Door and it's all wrong. Smaller than Room and emptier and it smells weird… It's gone darker."

This poignant novel reminded me that it is important to reflect on our exile from Jerusalem from the perspective of the people who experienced it—not just the suffering and horror stories, but the adjustment from Room to Outside.

Room opened for the Children of Israel on the 17th of Tammuz, when the Babylonians breached the walls of Jerusalem. Their Room was a tiny walled city, the center of their universe. Kings came and went. Invaders attacked, failed, and left. Room remained a safe world throughout it all.

Life in their Room could not have been easy. Jerusalem was not in an agricultural area and it was not on any major trade routes. It was our Room only because it was Jerusalem, the home of the Beit HaMikdash. Three weeks after Room was opened, the Temple was destroyed and Room's inhabitants were introduced to Outside.

None of us would question whether Jack was better off Outside, with medical care, regular food, clothes, playgrounds, and other people. It's shocking to read how unsafe Jack and even Ma felt Outside, and yet we finally appreciate the intense challenge of leaving Room for Outside.

The world opened for the ancient Israelites when they were exiled from Jerusalem. Their lives had been harsh and brutal. For years, faraway kings and armies had brought chaos and misfortune. But Jerusalem was their Room. It took them time to adjust to living a far richer life in Babylon, Persia, and eventually all over the globe.

Life in the United States is better for a Jew than life in pre-WWII Europe. The ghettos were our Rooms, and it took us time to adjust to Outside. No matter how harsh a world it was, it was difficult to lose Room. All the rules are different. The Jewish immigrants were as confused as Jack about what was real and what was not.

Should we focus on how much we lost when Room opened? Shall we mourn over how much has changed because we no longer have our Room?

I suspect that the Three Weeks of Mourning that begin with the 17th of Tammuz, from the opening of Room till the destruction of the Temple, are for us to focus on our adjustment to Outside: How much of Room did we take with us? Was the loss of Room a painful transitional adjustment to something better? What of Room do we miss?

Are we trying to recreate Room in Outside?

Life in the Jerusalem Room was not a perfect environment, just as Jewish life in the cities and villages across Europe was not paradise. When the walls of our Room were breached, we had an opportunity to consider which parts of Room we would take with us to Outside.

I wonder what I would have chosen to take.

God knows that our Diasporic communities have not been perfect, yet they are certainly preferable to our far more limited and isolated households. We have spent so long missing Outside that I wonder how many of us have considered how difficult it will be to leave our Rooms. Our isolation has come with devastating challenges. We know how much we need Outside, just as Jack did. Unfortunately, after so long away from these necessities, we have grown accustomed to life without them. When the time comes to return Outside, will we be ready? I think that we will need to take extreme care to sensitively navigate our emotional needs.

What are we going to leave behind? What will we choose to take?

KINAH 19

Shame

"Oh my soul... be prepared for him who knows how to ask questions."

—T.S. Eliot

"Hashem Elokim called out to the man and said to him, 'Where are you?' He said, 'I heard the sound of You in the Garden, and I was afraid because I am naked, so I hid.' And He said, 'Who told you that you are naked? Have you eaten of the tree from which I commanded you not to eat?"

—Bereishit 3:9–11

"Yours, my Master, is the righteousness... And ours is the shamefacedness..."

"I was afraid," not, "I was ashamed."

When Adam and Ḥavah were created, "they were both naked ... and they were not ashamed" (Bereishit 2:25). Once they ate the fruit of the Tree of Knowledge, they saw their nakedness through newly opened eyes, and so they "sewed together a fig leaf and made themselves aprons" (Bereishit 3:7). Once Adam and Ḥavah covered themselves, their shame disappeared. They had never felt shame for their transgression, only for their nakedness.

Perhaps they could have responded, "Yours, our Master, is the righteousness, and ours is the shamefacedness," and things would have developed differently.

This kinah is our opportunity to recreate that moment in Eden and respond as Adam *should* have. We will "be prepared for him who knows how to ask questions." A simple step that can repair worlds.

This time period of being in quarantine has afforded us an opportunity to consider the things about which we are not proud. We have an opportunity to take a close look at our prayer, at the way we relate to those closest to us, at our *ḥesed*, and at our *middos* development. Perhaps instead of using quarantine as a way of "hiding behind a tree," we can use quarantine as of way of stepping out and saying to God, "Yours is the righteousness, and ours is the embarrassment."

What Could Have Been

Beowulf, son of Ecgtheow, said: "I had a fixed purpose when I put to sea. As I sat in the boat with my band of men, I meant to perform to the uttermost what your people wanted or perish the attempt, in the fiend's clutches. And I shall fulfill that purpose, prove myself with a proud deed or meet my death here in the mead hall."

God took a nation from the midst of another with miracles. He redeemed a nation for Himself. He designated us witnesses to His divinity. He allowed us to taste the honey-sweet biscuits. He sustained us with manna, and the well, and the pillar of cloud. He ensured that we lacked nothing in the desert. He granted us victory against Siçhon and Og, sent us the fourteen judges, gave us a Mishkan and Beit HaMikdash…

When God did all of these things for us, we intended to accomplish great things. Yet, just like the legendary Beowulf, we did not live up to the challenges we accepted upon ourselves. For this, and in this, we say, "With You, God, is the right, and the shame is on us" (Daniel 4:34).

This kinah addresses all that could have been for the Jewish people, if only they had taken advantage of God's many gifts. If they had lived up to their commitments, they could have reached astonishing heights. This forces us to ask ourselves: Are we living up to *our* commitments?

I wonder What Could Have Been had Cain responded positively to God's Voice, "If you improve just a little, you will elevate the world!"

I wonder What Could Have Been had Jacob climbed the ladder in his dream.

I wonder What Could Have Been and What Could Be had we heard, and if we would hear, all of God's invitations to rise to greatness.

KINAH 20

Piercing the Clouds

"Incline Your ear, my God, to the licentious ones who blaspheme saying, 'Whom do I have to fear in heaven?'"

One of the major themes in *Eichah* and Tisha B'Av is, "You wrapped Yourself in a cloud that no prayer can pierce" (Eichah 3:44). As we discussed in our preparatory thoughts, our prayers are blocked by God's Cloud (see "The Futility of Our Words).

Rabbi Akiva was standing in trial before Tineus Rufus. Yehoshua the grits-dealer stood with him in prayer. A cloud descended and enveloped them. Yehoshua said, "It seems to me that the cloud has descended and enveloped us only that the rabbi's prayer should not be heard" (Eichah Rabba 3:44).

As long as we have prayer, we have hope. When God Himself blocks our prayers, we lose all hope. In this kinah we wonder, "If God ignores the blasphemy of our enemies, how can we believe that He hears our prayers?"

We empower our prayers to pierce the clouds by arguing not for ourselves, but for God's Glory. We want God to silence those who deny Him. Once the skies are opened to that prayer, the others will rise up with them.

It is not enough to pray for ourselves as individuals. It may not even be enough to pray for our communities. Let us pray for the entire Jewish people and the entire world. Let us pray for all of Creation to glorify His Name. If we find ways to honor Hashem with actions that we can perform within our homes, perhaps He will give us the chance.

KINAH 21

The Greatness of a Human Being

"Terror rolls over me, pursues my path like the wind, and my rescue like a cloud passes on" (Iyov 30:15). You chase as the wind the men who are noble hearted and who should be the instruments of my deliverance. You scatter and make to pass as clouds the men who are noble hearted and through whom salvation should come to me; as it is said, "How has my Master covered the daughter of Zion with a cloud in His anger, and cast down from heaven to earth the beauty of Israel, and remembered not His footstool in the day of His anger?" (Eicha 2:1)

—Midrash Eichah 1.1.21

Kinah 21 describes the Roman martyrdom of the Ten Sages in the second century. We lament that Hashem deprived us of the very people who could have led us to salvation.

I often wonder why the Romans allowed the Israelites such direct access while they were torturing and murdering our great rabbis. It seems that the Romans wanted us to see our leaders as ordinary human beings who, when suffering, were no different from the rest of us.

What the Romans failed to understand is that our rabbis' humanity was the very reason that we connected with them in the first place. The Sages did not represent an unrealistic transcendence of the human experience. The Sages represented the inspiring heights that *every* human being can ascend. We do not mourn the loss of leaders with extraordinary powers. We mourn the loss of *gedolim* who can show us by example what we all have the potential to become.

A nation that can live with the awareness of human potential will find the key to salvation. This time, the cloud that covered Zion was our confusion and despair. Confusion sets in if we begin to see our leaders as inaccessibly powerful instead of ordinary human beings who achieved greatness. We despair if we stop believing that we can find the key to salvation within ourselves.

Nowadays, we cannot always trust our communal leaders. Sometimes, people in power do not know or make the right decisions for our collective safety, wellbeing, and growth. They are just like the rest of us—vulnerable, afraid, and suffering. They, like us, have the potential to make wise and righteous choices, especially if we help them understand our needs. But we, too, have potential. We can look to other people for inspiration, be they leaders or family, ancestors or friends. We must also look inward, at our own potential, and do our best to be a model for others.

Just as we suffer together, we can inspire together. We can give each other strength, hope, and clarity—so long as we always remember that every single one of us can reach great heights. The key to salvation lies within us all.

KINAH 23

A Fight for Dignity

The young Rabbi Yishmael was saved because he maintained his connection to God and Torah while imprisoned in Rome. His commitment lived on in his son and daughter, who refused to dishonor their kohanic lineage, even in the face of death, as told in Gittin 58a:

> *Rabbi Yehoshua ben Ḥananiah once happened to go to the great city of Rome, and he was told there that there was in the prison a Jewish child with beautiful eyes and face and curly locks.*
>
> *He went and stood at the doorway of the prison and said, "Who gave Yaakov for a spoil and Yisrael to the robbers?" (Yeshayahu 42:24). The child answered, "Is it not God, He against whom we have transgressed and in whose ways they would not walk, neither were they obedient unto his law?" (Ibid.).*
>
> *He said, "I feel sure that this one will be a teacher in Israel. I swear that I will not budge from here before I ransom him, whatever price may be demanded. It is reported that he*

did not leave the spot before he had ransomed him at a high figure, nor did many days pass before he became a teacher in Israel. And who was he? He was Rabbi Yishmael ben Elisha."

Rav Yehudah said in the name of Rav, "It is related that the son and the daughter of Rabbi Yishmael ben Elisha were carried off [and sold] to two masters."

After some time, the two [Roman masters] met together. One said, "I have a slave, whose beauty is in all the world." The other said, "I have a female slave, whose beauty is unmatched in all the world." They said, "Let us marry them to one another and share the children."

They put them in the same room. The son sat in one corner and the daughter in another.

He said, "I am a priest descended from High Priests. Shall I marry a bondwoman?"

She said, "I am a priestess descended from High Priests. Shall I be married to a slave?" So they wept through all the night.

When the day dawned, they recognized one another. They fell on one another's necks and bemoaned themselves with tears until their souls departed.

For them, Yirmiyahu lamented, "For these I am weeping, mine eye, mine eye drops water" (Eicha 1:16).

Jerusalem lay in ruins. The Temple had been destroyed. Rabbi Yishmael's children were slaves in Rome, yet they would not let go of their ancestral legacy. They risked their lives to preserve the *kehunah*, which still waits, almost two thousand years later, to assume its proper role in God's home. What a devastating loss.

We are constantly bombarded with messages that contradict our laws, values, and dignity. We hear leaders urging us to maintain halacha, and of course it is important to do so. Yet Rabbi Yishmael's children do not speak of law, but of dignity. "I am a child of Avraham, Yitzhak, and Yaakov; shall I lower myself to act in such a manner?" They died preserving the dignity of Israel and the *kehunah*.

When we demand observance without echoing the message of this young boy and girl, Yirmiyahu laments, "For these I am weeping, mine eye, mine eye drops water."

When we fail to inspire pride in our children, Yirmiyahu laments, "For these I am weeping, mine eye, mine eye drops water."

Jewish survival depends on more than halacha. Our commitment to observance is so much stronger when it comes from a place of honor. We must foster a sense of pride in our identities as Jews, for ourselves and for our children.

So too, throughout this pandemic, we have been bombarded with contradictory messages. Taking measures to protect ourselves and each other is not merely about following mandates. It is about maintaining our dignity.

This is a public health issue about a highly contagious disease. We cannot escape that every single one of us impacts our communal health. The world is watching how the Jewish people respond to this crisis. We are observing each other, if only from a distance. But even in our separate corners, we can see ourselves. We know what our *own* actions are. When we make decisions, let us remember what we are protecting. May our choices preserve our honor. May our honor bring about our survival.

KINAH 24

As Angels

This kinah, by Rabbi Elazar HaKalir, focuses on yet another tragic aspect of the Temple's destruction. Not only was the Temple edifice destroyed, but its furnishings, adornments, and holy vessels were plundered. Each of these components was designed to reflect the celestial Temple in the Heavens Above, where the ministering angels offer their fiery and awesome pæans to the Almighty. Each component also corresponded to a particular natural phenomenon.

Here we lament that these adornments and vessels were ignominiously vandalized by Nebuchadnezzar and sent to adorn pagan temples in the Babylonian Empire. Here we mourn the degradation of both the terrestrial and celestial Temples. Here we grieve over the diminution of benefits derived from the phenomena of nature (ArtScroll Kinot 264).

One of the most prolific writers of responsa was Rabbi David ibn Abi Zimra (1479–1573), also known as the Radbaz. As a Kabbalist, Radbaz maintained that there are profound, mystical meanings behind the plain meaning of the Scripture. Yet one questioner asked Radbaz to explain Adam's sin according to its plain, non-Kabbalistic meaning (Responsum 256). Adam was God's creation, the work of His Hands. The rabbis wax eloquent about the loftiness of his spirituality. All that God commanded Adam was to not eat from a single tree—surely a small matter! How could he have yielded to Ḥavah's importunities and defy his God?

Radbaz observed that the Zohar has tremendous things to say on this subject, but he was not permitted to divulge them; and in any event, the questioner wanted the *pshat*, not a mystical interpretation. He proceeded to expound his simple reading of the text: Adam knew that the fruit of the Tree of Life could grant him immortality. Without this fruit, Adam would be subject to the same law of decay as all earthly creatures. But Adam wished to live forever so that he could praise God for all eternity. He aspired to reach the level of the angels—possibly even higher. He wanted to discover where the Tree of Life was situated in the Garden, for this information had not been imparted to him.

When Ḥavah ate the fruit of the Tree of Knowledge, Adam saw her knowledge increase and sought to do the same. He realized that the Tree of Knowledge would endow him the wisdom to discover the Tree of Life. He knew that its fruit was forbidden, but he justified his transgression by his sublime motivations. Furthermore, he believed he could repent and erase his sin once he attained his spiritual ambition. Adam did sin, but at least his motives were righteous, worthy of his elevated level. Unfortunately, after he ate the forbidden fruit, he did not repent, and he was so powerfully impacted by his exile that he lost his connection to his greatness.

Perhaps we cannot understand, appreciate, or even relate to the idea that our earthly Temple mirrored the angels' celestial Temple. However, we can respect that a person may aspire to live closer to God than even the highest angels.

We lost much of this drive to connect Heaven and Earth when the Temple was destroyed. We should aim high, as Adam did, without repeating his mistakes. How can we bring the spiritual realm to our material world? How can we elevate our material actions to spiritual heights? Even within our own homes, we can touch the Heavens. We do not need immortality to follow Hashem's mitzvot and sing His praises. Should we really be as angels, or should we be as Man, ascending the heights that God already gives us the opportunities to ascend?

KINAH 26

As Parents for Children

This kinah is based on *Eichah Rabbah*, Introduction 24:

> *There and then, Yirmiyahu went to the Cave of Machpelah and said to the Patriarchs of the world, "Arise, for the time has come when your presence is required before the Holy One, Benedicted is He."*
>
> *They said to him, "For what purpose?"*
>
> *He answered, "I know not," because he was afraid, lest they say, "In your lifetime has such a thing happened to my children!"*
>
> *Yirmiyahu left them, stood by the banks of the Jordan, and called out, "Son of Amram, son of Amram, arise, the time has come when your presence is required before the Holy One, Benedicted is He."*
>
> *Moshe said to Yirmiyahu, "How is this day different from other days that my presence is required before the Holy One, Benedicted is He?"*

Yirmiyahu replied, "I know not."

Did Moshe and the Patriarchs live in their graves, that they needed to be summoned thence to come before God?

We can find a hint in the following Responsum of the Rashba: A questioner asked why we pray to "the God of Avraham, the God of Yitzḥak, and the God of Yaakov,' and not "the God Who created heaven and earth." The Rashba replies that this expresses a profound idea from the saying, "The Patriarchs are the Divine Chariot" (Bereishit Rabbah 82:6).

According to the *pshat*, the reason we begin our prayers by invoking the Patriarchs is that Moshe did so (Shemot 32:13). God said to Moshe, "I am the God of your father, the God of Avraham, the God of Yitzḥak, and the God of Yaakov" (Shemot 3:6). He did not say, "I am the God Who created Heaven and Earth." Furthermore, we are human beings and our prayers are for the satisfaction of human needs. It is right for us to begin our prayers with a reference to our finest models of humanity.

There are times when we call on our patriarchs and Moshe as their children and students. We are not appealing to their spirituality or heroism. We approach them on a very human level. Yirmiyahu called on them to appear before God as parents arguing for their children. We hope that our human relationship with the Patriarchs and Moshe will stimulate a similar response from God as our Father and Rabbi.

This kinah is Yirmiyahu's advocacy as personified in the name of this Hebrew month, *Av*, meaning "father." He understood that our only hope lay in speaking to God, not as the Creator of Heaven and Earth, not as the Giver of the Torah, but as our Parent and Rabbi—our Av.

The current crisis has transformed our family dynamics. Many households have transitioned from having one stay-at-home parent to two. Newly homebound fathers and mothers should have a much deeper appreciation of stay-at-home parents, who are all too often taken for granted.

It is wonderful if families can cherish this time together, using it to strengthen their relationships. They may feel grateful, especially when others must endure these times alone. That said, it is understandable for anyone to have strained relationships with their housemates. Parenthood may sometimes feel more like a burden than a privilege. These are extraordinary circumstances with extraordinary challenges, particularly for parents of school-aged children, who may find themselves more directly positioned as teachers.

The Coronavirus pandemic is a formative experience for our younger generations. This is their Pearl Harbor, their 9/11, their living history. How will the children of today call on their parents? How will their parents answer them?

KINAH 27

Allegories & Numbers

Men of sound intellect and probity,
Weigh with good understanding what lies hidden
Behind the veil of strange allegory.

—Dante Alighieri, *Inferno*

The wisdom of the past was hidden and preserved in popular customs, stories, children's games, legends, traditions, and seemingly innocuous books. This kinah speaks to us through allegory and numbers. It challenges us to use our "sound intellect and probity" to discover what lies behind the veil of its allegory.

Many of the kinot also use numbers in their structure and message. (This was once a common tool: Each one of the three parts of the Divine Comedy, quoted above, has exactly thirty-three cantos. Each canto has exactly 115 or 160 lines, the sum of whose digits is seven.) This lament uses numbers to draw us into the powerful scene that lies at its core:

> *As Yirmiyahu departed from the Temple, he met a filthy woman of beautiful features. "I command you, in the name of God and man, to reveal whether you are one of the demons or of humankind."*

145

"I am neither demon, nor worthless lump of clay. I am the spirit of the Jewish people, the daughter of one and of three, my offspring number sixty with one from twelve and seventy-one!"

The numbers represent the One God, the three patriarchs, the "sixty ten-thousands" who left Egypt, the twelve tribes, and the seventy-one souls to enter Egypt. As to the allegory, Yirmiyahu was walking away from the smoldering ruins of the Temple. How filthy was this beautiful woman for a prophet to ask if she was a demon or human? How many corpses had he seen? How many broken, twisted bodies? How many atrocities did he witness during the siege?

It could not have been the woman's filth that caught the prophet's attention. No matter how dirty she was, he had seen much worse. Rather, he notices her beautiful features showing through the filth. How could she retain such striking beauty under such horrible conditions?

Thus, she becomes an allegory for Am Yisrael. How would they survive? How could anyone maintain his or her beauty in exile? Would Israel sacrifice her beauty in Babylon? Would she lose her humanity in the name of survival?

I'm sure that many of us wonder how we will survive this pandemic. Even for those who are blessed with a safe place to stay, live-in loved ones, a reliable source of income, healthful food, adequate exercise, intellectual enrichment, emotional care, and communal engagement... we all know that these circumstances are not ideal. We yearn to eventually return to normalcy. It is one thing to sustain our lives; it is another to sustain the human spirit. All we can do is focus on the beauty beneath the filth, and hopefully we shall remain beautiful ourselves. The Spirit of Israel connects us to each other and our roots, reminding us to see our indomitable courage, magnificence, and strength.

KINAH 31

Daughters of Exiles

*Rabbi Abba bar Kahana opened his
discourse with the verse, "Let out your voice
with joy, O daughter of Gallim" (Yeshayahu
10:30). Yeshayahu said to Israel, "Rather
than uttering songs and praises in worship of
the stars, sing the words of Torah with a
joyous voice, sing in the synagogues with a
joyous voice."*

*O daughter of Gallim, as the waves are
conspicuous in the sea, so are the Patriarchs
in the world. Another interpretation of "bat
Gallim" (בַּת גַלִּים) is to read the text as "bat
Golim" (בַּת גּוֹלִים), daughters of exiles:
Daughter of Avraham, of whom it is written,
"And there was a famine in the land, and
Avraham went down into Egypt" (Bereishit
12:10); daughter of Yitzḥak, of whom it is
written, "And Yitzḥak went unto Avimelech,
King of the Philistines, onto Gerar" (26:1);
daughter of Yaakov, of whom it is written,
"And he went to Paddan-Aram" (28:5).*

—Introduction to *Eichah Rabbah*

Rabbi Abba is saying that we, the Daughters of Exiles, should let out our voices in joyous songs of Torah and service of God. We can learn from the Patriarchs how to sing even in exile. The Patriarchs found ways to use their time to their advantage. They each acquired great wealth, achieved new heights, and enhanced their reputations. They became the masters of their situations, because even when forced to leave their homes, they continued to live and sing with joy.

The Jewish people have suffered terribly in our millennia of exile, yet somehow, we have thrived. We produced countless Torah works. We maintained our commitment to Israel with such passion that we were able to return, rebuild the land, and revive the language. No matter how much we suffered, we continued singing.

Throughout our history, we have had many inspiring Daughters of the Singing Exiles. The concentration camp inmates who risked their lives to light Ḥanukah candles were Daughters of the Singing Exiles. The Russian and Polish Jews who dressed as royalty every Shabbos, no matter how poor or desperate, were Daughters of the Singing Exiles. The Sephardim exiled from Spain, who built new and vibrant communities all over the world, were Daughters of the Singing Exiles. Rav Breuer and the Satmar Rav, who arrived in America as older men and built their respective communities after the Holocaust, were Daughters of the Singing Exiles.

Rabbi Abba understood that Diasporic Jews reading Yirmiyahu's words would be tempted to sing with the other nations, to turn to gods and cultures that were not their own. They would be attracted to a life of singing, of joy without exile. Rabbi Abba reminds them and us that the real singer can sing even in times of suffering, who has song in her heart and soul, who can emulate the Singing Exiles.

This Tisha B'Av, we find ourselves exiled to our own homes. Have we emulated our Patriarchs by using this time to our advantage? Do we learn and engage with ideas? Do we cultivate careers and nurture relationships? Do we work on our hobbies and develop our skills? Do we strengthen our Yiddishkeit and help our communities?

We are the Daughters of Exile. No matter how much we suffer, our hearts and souls continue singing. Let us raise our voices in joyous song together.

KINAH 34

Should We Forgive Our Enemies?

This kinah is based on the tragic descent of King Yeho'ash and the murder of the prophet Zechariah.

When Yeho'ash was only a baby, his father was killed and his grief-stricken grandmother massacred their entire family. The Kohen Gadol, Yehoyada, rescued the infant and hid him inside the Beit HaMikdash. Yeho'ash was raised in the *Kodesh Kedoshim*, the Holy of Holies—the place that could only be safely entered by the holiest man on the holiest of days. He did not leave until he assumed the throne at age seven.

Initially, Yeho'ash is glowingly described: "All his days, Yeho'ash did what was pleasing in the eyes of Hashem, as instructed by Yehoyada the Kohen Gadol" (II Melachim 12:3). Then Yehoyada died and Yeho'ash went astray. The people treated him like a god. The Temple became a place of idol worship. The prophets tried and failed to restore the kingdom. "The spirit of God enveloped Zechariah, son of Yehoyada the Kohen Gadol," who admonished the people (II Divrei HaYamim 24:17).

Yeho'ash responded appallingly: He ordered the people to stone Zechariah. He disregarded Yehoyada's *hesed*, showing no loyalty to the man who saved him and raised

151

him, who is called "his father" in this very verse (II Divrei HaYamim 24:22). Yeho'ash killed Zechariah, Yehoyada's own son, on the very Temple grounds where Yehoyada once saved his life. Zechariah's blood remained in the Temple courtyard, bubbling and boiling, for 150 years. It was a sign that the evil act committed in this sacred place would not go unanswered.

The Gemara recounts how Nevuzaradan, Nevuchadnetzar's captain of the guard, fought his way into the Temple. He slaughtered 2,110,000 Israelites, hacking through the generations that had ignored Zechariah's blood. Nevuzaradan saw the still-boiling blood on the Temple floor and demanded an explanation. Under threat of torture, the people of Jerusalem confessed: "There was a prophet among us who used to rebuke us, and we rose up against him and killed him, and for many years his blood has not rested" (Gittin 57b).

Nevuzaradan tried to "appease" Zechariah. He slaughtered the men of the Great Sanhedrin and the Lesser Sanhedrin. The blood did not settle. He slew young men and virgins. The blood did not settle. He murdered young schoolchildren. The blood did not settle. Finally, when Nevurazadan had slain 94,000 people, he stopped and cried out. "Zechariah, Zechariah, I have destroyed the worthy among them! Do You desire me to massacre them all?" (Sanhedrin 96b). Instantly, the blood stopped boiling. Nevurazadan asked himself, "If they, who only killed one person, have been so severely punished, what will be my fate?" So he fled, sent a deed to his house, and became a convert.

How did the Rabbinic Court react when they recognized the supplicant before them as the genocidal Nevuzaradan? Did they have the right to authorize such a conversion? How did the Israelites feel when he was called to the Torah as Nevuzaradan the son of our Patriarch Avraham? Did anyone invite him for Shabbos dinner? Was it Nevuzaradan who reached for greatness, or was it the people who granted him some degree of absolution through their acceptance?

This is not our only account of an enemy proselyte. As we discussed in Kinah 8, the Gemara relates a legend about Nero, who'd been sent from Rome to attack Jerusalem (see "As Swift as Eagles"). Nero asked a child to share a verse that he'd recently learned. The child bravely recited, "And I will lay vengeance upon Edom (Rome) by the hand of My people Israel" (Yeḥezkel 25:14). Nero, not wanting to be God's scapegoat, ran away and became a convert, and Rabbi Meir was descended from him (Gittin 56a).

The rare enemy who seeks forgiveness continues, millennia later, to challenge us. In *The Sunflower*, Simon Wiesenthal writes of an incident that occurred when he was a concentration camp inmate. One day, his work detail was sent to an army hospital for wounded German soldiers. A nurse approached Simon and asked if he was a Jew. When he affirmed that he was, she took him to the bedside of a young, fatally wounded Nazi named Karl. Karl's head was completely covered in bandages, with openings only for his mouth, nose, and ears. He was resigned to death, but he felt the need to confess a particular experience that haunted him: When the German army sent Karl to Russia, he was ordered to partake in a pogrom. He and his fellow SS officers forced hundreds of Jews into a house, mostly women and elderly men. They set the house ablaze with grenades and burned the Jews alive, shooting anyone who tried to escape.

"I saw a man with a small child in his arms. His clothes were alight. By his side stood a woman, doubtless the mother of the child. With his free hand the man covered the child's eyes... then he jumped into the street. Seconds later the mother followed... Oh God!" cried Karl. "I don't know how many tried to jump out of the windows but that one family I shall never forget—least of all the child."

Later, in the trenches of Crimea, Karl could not bring himself to fire his weapon. He suddenly envisioned that burning family and thought, "I cannot shoot them a second time." At that moment, a bombshell exploded next to him, blinding him and destroying his body. Yet nothing was worse than the pain of his conscience. The only way he could die in peace, he beseeched Simon, was if a Jew forgave him.

Simon left the room without a word. When he returned the next day, the nurse told him that Karl had died.

For years, Simon pondered the morality of his decision. As he explains, "The crux of the matter is, of course, the question of forgiveness. Forgetting is something that time alone takes care of, but forgiveness is an act of volition." He does not ask if our enemies deserve forgiveness. He asks if we must forgive our enemies.

Of course, we do distinguish between our most terrible enemies and the ordinary people in our lives. The Gemara relates Rav Neḥunya's praise of Mar Zutra, who would say before going to bed, "I forgive anyone who has vexed me" (Megillah 28a). The Mishnah Berurah suggests that a person who forgives anyone who wrongs them will attain long life (239:I:9). Some people recite this introduction to *Kri'at Shema Al HaMita*, the Bedtime Shema:

> *Master of the Universe! I hereby forgive anyone who angered or antagonized me, or who transgressed against me—whether against my body, my property, my honor, or anything that is mine; whether under duress or willfully, whether unintentionally or purposefully; whether through speech, deed, thought or passion, whether in this incarnation or another incarnation—I forgive every Jew. May no person be punished because of me.*

> *May it be Your will, Hashem, my God and the God of my forefathers, that I transgress no more. Whatever transgressions I have done before You, may You blot out in Your abundant mercies, but not through suffering or terrible illnesses...*

Yet these verses do not account for personal accountability and teshuvah. Forgiveness is often a form of compassion, but it is not always appropriate or emotionally healthful.

Forgiving someone who has not changed, who actively endangers you, does not help anyone. Forgiving someone who expresses a desire to change, who cares about you and your community, can pave the way for peace and mutual growth.

This kinah describes how the earth would not cover Zechariah's blood until the sword of the tormentors avenged him. Boiling blood, or the expression "it makes my blood boil," connotes anger—often at people, events, or conditions beyond one's control. "There's no disinfectant at the store." "My neighbor walked near me without a protective mask!" "I've been on hold for hours and I still haven't spoken to customer service." "What will my kids do all summer without camp?"

When a lack of safety results in illness and death, who should we forgive, if anyone? If the country lacks resources for our psychological and financial needs, who should we forgive, if anyone? If the strain of the pandemic is too much for us, who should we forgive, if anyone?

Can we always forgive those who wronged us? *Should* we? Depending on the circumstance, either choice may be acceptable. As Simon Wiesenthal writes, forgiveness is "an act of volition" (*The Sunflower*). We have the freedom to forgive and the freedom to deny forgiveness. Simply having that choice and even the ability to choose can help us move forward in our lives. And just as we should stand up for ourselves and our people, we should always look for a course of action that will bring us closer together. With a balance of *ḥesed* and *gevurah*, we can survive and come out of this beautifully, stronger than ever before.

KINAH 45

Empty Spaces

Rabban Gamliel, Rabbi Elazar ben Azariah, Rabbi Yehoshua, and Rabbi Akiva were coming up to Jerusalem together, and just as they came to Mount Scopus, they saw a fox emerging from the Holy of Holies. The Sages fell weeping, yet Rabbi Akiva seemed merry.

"Why are you merry?" they said to him.

"Why are you weeping?" said he.

They said to him, "This is the place of which it was said, 'And the common man that draws near shall die,' and it is now the haunt of foxes. Should we not weep?"

He said to them, "Therefore, am I merry. For it is written, 'And I will take to Me faithful witnesses to record, Uriah the priest and Zechariah ben Yevarecheyhu.' Now, what is the connection between Uriah and Zechariah? Uriah prophesied during the first Temple period, while Zechariah prophesied during the second Temple period. But Scripture connected the later prophecy of Zechariah with the earlier prophecy of

Uriah. It is written in the prophecy of Uriah, 'Therefore shall Zion for your sake be ploughed as a field.' It is written in Zechariah, 'Thus says the God of Hosts, there shall yet old men and old women sit in the broad places of Jerusalem.' So long as Uriah's prophecy had not had its fulfilment, I had misgivings that Zechariah's prophecy might not be fulfilled. Now that Uriah's prophecy has been fulfilled, it is quite certain that Zechariah's prophecy will be fulfilled.

Said they to him, "Akiva, you have comforted us! Akiva, you have comforted us!"

—Makkot 24b

I experience a different feeling in my gut when I see an empty space where a synagogue once stood than when I see a synagogue that stands empty.

There used to be a synagogue on Rivington near Ludlow, on the Lower East Side. I first saw the building when it was abandoned. It is no longer there. The street corner is named for the congregation's longtime rabbi, but the sign is rarely noticed and it serves as no more than a plaque proclaiming that a synagogue once stood here.

When I saw the empty building, I could imagine filling it again with the sounds of Jewish life. I began picturing a vibrant center with classes and social programs. Even an empty building holds promise. There is currently an empty lot where hundreds of families once joined for prayer, holidays, weddings, classes, and great events. The now-empty lot is nowhere near large enough to contain all the tears that were shed on that spot. That valuable piece of real-estate cannot begin to approach the priceless prayers that were offered in that place.

If all the souls that found succor in the synagogue were piled one atop the other in that empty lot, they would reach the Heavens. I doubt that a library could contain all the sermons, classes, and words of Torah that were spoken in that shul. The vacuum in its place is far greater than the building that once stood there and any building that will eventually replace it.

A synagogue is more than its physical space. The ruins of a once-vibrant congregation at least offered a connection to the great achievements of the its founders, members, and rabbis. But now, there is nothing left. A small apartment building next to the empty lot has a stone arch with "Talmud Torah" engraved on it. The arch does not strike me in the gut with as much violence as that empty lot.

Abandonment hurts. Demolishment hurts more. What about the synagogues that were turned into churches? We need not travel to Poland to find such places. They are all over New York. You can find them in Harlem and the Bronx. My sister-in-law lives across the street from an apartment building in Montreal which has stained glass windows gracing bathrooms and bedrooms from the time it was a shul.

The rabbis were more distressed by the fox running through the area of the Holy of Holies than the ruins of the Temple: "This is the place of which it was said, 'And the common man that draws near shall die,' and it is now the haunt of foxes. Should we not weep?"

It once was that anyone who entered the Holy of Holies improperly, even the Kohen Gadol on Yom Kippur, would immediately die. Now even a wild animal can run there without fear. The holiest place on earth has lost its sanctity. How can sanctity disappear? What about all the offerings made there? Did the service of the Kohen Gadol leave no mark? Is it possible that all those prayers are gone?

The first three rabbis saw the empty lot and wept. Rabbi Akiva saw the same empty lot and saw *life*. He perceived the seeds of redemption in the emptiness—the lost sanctity. He read Zechariah's prophecy and found a promise: What once existed in that place was gathered up on high, treasured, and protected. The countless Temple offerings and prayers are still there in spirit, free of physical boundaries and limitations. The physical loss will someday be restored. In the meantime, the spiritual accomplishments live in the words of the prophets and in the Hand of God.

The empty space of the Holy of Holies is not empty. It is *transparent*. The memory and sanctity of our people remain, and if we cannot see it, we can feel it.

We weep and mourn over the horrific devastation that took place on Tisha B'Av. Yet we never forget the prayers, Torah, and mitzvot of the countless victims of pogroms, the Crusades, and the Holocaust. Our people's *tefillot*, Torah, and mitzvot live on even today. We weep because we yearn for a world that is great enough to contain them.

Each time we pray the same words as those millions of Jews across the centuries and around the world, we declare that their prayers live.

Each time we study the same words of Torah as those millions of Jews across the centuries and around the world, we declare that their Torah lives.

Each time we observe the same mitzvot as those millions of Jews across the centuries and around the world, we declare that their mitzvot live.

Each time we chant the same Kinot as those millions of Jews across the centuries and around the world, we declare our determination to live. It is up to us to build a world great enough to contain and reflect all those prayers, all those words of Torah, all those mitzvot.

Our shuls may be empty now. Our communities may seem deserted. Our losses may strike a deep, painful chord in our hearts. But we are still here. We are a living people. We are memory, we are courage, we are hope. We are life, and in life, there is comfort.

Made in the USA
San Bernardino, CA
14 July 2020

75490771R00100